MAN OF PEACE

MAN OF PEACE

Pope Pius XII

MARGHERITA MARCHIONE

Paulist Press
New York/Mahwah, N.J.

Cover and book design by Lynn Else

Photographic references
Pontifical Museum and Gallery Monuments, Vatican City; Archives:
Archdiocese of Baltimore and St. Paul–Minneapolis, Diocese of Trenton, New
Jersey; Religious Teachers Filippini, Catholic University of America
(Manuscripts Collection); Fordham (David Berns Archives), Notre Dame and
Seton Hall University (Special Collections).

Acknowledgments
The author thanks Maria Fede Caproni for research assistance.
She is grateful to Ralph M. Cestone for the financial assistance given
for this publication.

Originally published 2002 by Libreria Editrice Vaticana
as a larger edition under the title
Shepherd of Souls: A Pictorial Life of Pope Pius XII

This edition published in 2003 by
Paulist Press
997 Macarthur Boulevard
Mahwah, New Jersey 07430

www.paulistpress.com

Library of Congress Cataloging-in-Publication Data

Marchione, Margherita.
Man of peace : Pope Pius XII / Margherita Marchione.
    p. cm.
Rev. ed. of: Shepherd of souls.
Includes bibliographical references (p.   ).
ISBN 0-8091-4245-7
1. Pius XII, Pope, 1876–1958—Pictorial works.
I. Marchione, Margherita. Shepherd of souls. II. Title.
BX1378 .M263 2004
282'.092—dc22
                                          2003019283

Printed and bound in the United States of America

Contents

CONTENTS

Pius XII pleaded for peace: "Nothing is lost through peace; all can be lost through war" (August 24, 1939). He denounced the war and emphasized reconciliation and a new internal order among the various nations on Christmas Eve 1942. He revealed that "hundreds of thousands of people, through no fault of theirs, sometimes only because of nationality or race, were destined to die."

PREFACE

Nearly half a century ago, as a seminarian beginning the study of theology, I shared in the excitement of a great rally in St. Peter's Square. More than a hundred thousand enthusiastic members of Catholic Action were there to hear and to cheer Pope Pius XII.

To this day I remember the drama of the Pope's sweeping gestures and the sense of marvel that he could deliver a long message without a text at hand. Long before the day of the teleprompter, he was able to draw upon the resources of a prodigious memory.

For many, Pope Pius XII was the enormously respected Church leader whose Christmas messages during and immediately after the Second World War prepared the way for democratic governments throughout much of Europe.

For others of us, including Pope John Paul II, he was also the one who laid the foundations within the Catholic Church for the Second Vatican Council. His encyclical on the Church as the Mystical Body of Christ *(Mystici Corporis Christi)*, 1943, opened the way for a new Catholic approach, to a theology grounded in the insights of both scripture scholars and theologians. The encyclical on biblical studies, *Divino Afflante Spiritu*, issued later in the same year, encouraged students of the written word of God to use fully the fruits of modern research. In *Mediator Dei*, 1947, Pope Pius XII set the stage for the full blossoming of the renewal of Catholic worship based on an accurate understanding of how the Church shaped its life of public prayer from the earliest Christian years. He took a first significant step in liturgical reform with the complete revision of the Holy Week Services of the Latin Church in 1956.

In addition, Pope Pius XII spoke out on many issues of moral concern and of public policy: these statements laid the foundations for the Second Vatican Council's Constitution *Gaudium et Spes,* on the Church in Today's World.

Certainly there is room for a wide range of informed, scholarly opinion on the record of any pontificate, especially one as long and as seriously challenged by chaotic and destructive world events as that of Pius XII. But we also need to remind ourselves that too often in our own history as a nation classic anti-Catholicism has expressed itself in attacks on the Papacy.

In these pages Sister Margherita takes us into the world of Pope Pius XII. She does so in a direct and readable way. She helps us to see how this Successor of Peter walked in the shoes of the Fisherman in troubling times with a faith that did not fail.

Cardinal William H. Keeler
Rome, October 27, 2001

FOREWORD

Man of Peace: Pope Pius XII, like the larger edition, *Shepherd of Souls: A Pictorial Life of Pope Pius XII*, describes the salient periods of Pius XII's pontificate and includes humorous anecdotes, historical facts, and human interest stories. It captures his role as spiritual leader of the Catholic Church and celebrates his accomplishments. It is a compelling, illustrated narrative that portrays the work of the Pontiff during World War I and World War II. In particular, it contains photographs and documents that reveal important issues of the Holocaust.

Sister Margherita Marchione's scholarship in the defense of Pope Pius XII began in 1997 when Paulist Press published *Yours Is a Precious Witness: Memoirs of Jews and Catholics in Wartime Italy*. This was followed by *Pope Pius XII: Architect for Peace* (2000) and *Consensus and Controversy: Defending Pope Pius XII* (2002). In response to the careless innuendos and malicious accusations that have been leveled against Pius XII, not only did she provide the testimony of Jews and Catholics, but she also has reproduced valuable Vatican documents that help our understanding of the Holocaust. Undoubtedly, *Shepherd of Souls: A Pictorial Life* of Pope Pius XII along with this abridged version, *Man of Peace: Pope Pius XII*, will help promote the truth about a saintly twentieth-century Pope.

Ralph M. Cestone

John Elliot is an internationally acclaimed, award-winning artist. He is listed in *Who's Who in the World* and *Who's Who in American Art*. His paintings are in numerous museums and private collections worldwide.

CHAPTER I

The Pacelli Family

The Pacelli family arrived in Rome in 1819 from the medieval village of Viterbo, Lazio. Pope Pius XII's grandfather, Marcantonio Pacelli, was invited to Rome by His Eminence Cardinal Caterini, his maternal uncle, to study canon law and serve the Church.

By 1851 he was made Undersecretary of the Interior by Pope Pius IX and was responsible for papal domains that stretched from the region of Emilia to Campania and across Italy from the Mediterranean to the Adriatic. Aware of the rapidly growing importance of the press, Marcantonio Pacelli co-founded *L'Osservatore Romano* in 1861. The newspaper became the voice of the Vatican. Today it continues to express the opinions of the Catholic Church.

Marcantonio was Undersecretary of the Interior until 1870, when the Italian government troops seized Rome after the annexation of the Papal States. This was the final step in the unification of Italy. Rome, the papal capital, now became the capital of the Italian Kingdom.

Under the "Law of Papal Guarantees" enacted in 1871, Pope Pius IX and his successors were guaranteed possession of St. Peter's, the Vatican and its gardens, the Lateran Palace, and the Villa of Castelgandolfo. Within these confines the Pope was granted sovereign rights, including the inviolability of his own person and the authority to receive and send ambassadors. He was also granted free use of the Italian telegraph, railway, and postal systems. However, Pius IX and his successors declined the annual subsidy and proclaimed themselves "prisoners of a usurping power."

Marcantonio had a close working relationship with Pope Pius IX until his death. He was present with his sons for the

Pope's funeral services. Eugenio was five years old and watched the procession bearing the corpse of Pius IX to the Church of San Lorenzo.

In October 1926, to eliminate the hostility between the Church and the nation of Italy, Prime Minister Benito Mussolini began negotiations which culminated in 1929 with the signing of the Lateran Treaty. The Church was given autonomous government and legislative power as well as the right to establish its own police force, civil service, postage services, flag, currency, radio station, and railway station. Among other concessions, papal churches, palaces, and other buildings outside the Vatican were given the territorial immunities normally reserved for foreign embassies. On February 11, 1929, Cardinal Pietro Gasparri, Vatican Secretary of State, and Mussolini signed the documents known as the Lateran Treaty. Eugenio Pacelli's brother Francesco, a brilliant Vatican lawyer, is credited with helping to negotiate the Lateran Treaty with the Italian Government.

The Signing of the Lateran Treaty of 1929.

Filippo Pacelli and the former Virginia Graziosi, Eugenio Pacelli's parents.

The Vatican was now an independent sovereign state. Pope Pius XI was pleased with the way the Treaty was written and stated: "We have given back God to Italy and Italy to God." Catholics throughout the world agreed with this assessment.

Early Years

The Pacelli family lived in a twelve-room apartment on the third floor of a four-story brownstone building called Palazzo Pediconi, across the Tiber from St. Peter's, at Number 34 Via degli Orsini, the palace built centuries earlier by the Orsini family.

Grandfather Marcantonio had seven children, of whom the third son was Filippo, who married Virginia Graziosi. They had four children. Eugenio, their second son and third child, became Pope Pius XII. The older Pacelli boy was Francesco. The two sisters were Giuseppina and Elisabetta. They and Francesco married distinguished Romans and had six children among them. Their offspring,

Eugenio at age seven.

ten grandnieces and grandnephews, were the children for whom a Christmas tree was arranged in the papal apartment, and their uncle, Pope Pius XII, gave them presents on Christmas Day.

Eugenio Maria Giuseppe Giovanni Pacelli was born in Rome, March 2, 1876, and baptized two days later, according to the records at the Church of Saints Celso and Giuliano. He was baptized by his uncle, Monsignor Giuseppe Pacelli. His godparents were his maternal uncle Filippo Graziosi and paternal aunt Teresa Pacelli.

A few years later, the Pacellis moved to Number 20 Via della Vetrina. Eugenio enjoyed a childhood in deeply religious surroundings. In the apartment there was a shrine of the Madonna with a prie-dieu where he would kneel and pray.

This new residence was fortunately nearer the kindergarten and elementary school conducted by the Sisters of Divine

A class picture of Eugenio and his brother, Filippo, at the elementary school of the Sisters of Divine Providence.

4

Providence. At age four Eugenio was enrolled in this school. In 1939, when a bust of Pius XII was unveiled at the school, the newly elected Pope took the opportunity to praise his loving mother and the devoted and gifted nuns for instilling in him the "first principles of Christian piety."

One day, his uncle, Monsignor Giuseppe Pacelli, told him the story of a missionary priest and martyr who was persecuted and finally crucified by his tormentors. Eugenio told his uncle that he too would like to be a martyr, "but—without the nails."

After kindergarten and elementary school, Eugenio began his studies at the Ennio Quirino Visconti Lyceum. It was here that he established a close friendship with a Jewish schoolmate, Guido Mendes. The boys visited each other's home and shared common interests. Still vivid in 1958 in the elderly Mendes's memory were the strong anti-Church and anti-clerical prejudices rampant among Italian schools and teachers in the 1890s. He remembered Eugenio always speaking up to defend the Church, and he described him as a careful dresser, always wearing a coat and tie, and distinguishing himself as the leading student. "He was always winning academic prizes," Mendes noted. He also recalled that when the Fascists began to threaten Jews in Italy, the then Secretary of State Pacelli helped the Mendes family flee to Jerusalem. They remained in touch with one another over the years.

Other classmates remember the time one of his professors asked the class to write an essay on the greatest leaders of all time. Eugenio wrote about Saint Augustine. The teacher was amused and asked ironically who could possibly make a case for Augustine, the self-confessed sinner. Pacelli stood up. "I can! Any time you are ready to listen. For one thing, the Bishop of Hippo repented." The teacher had no answer in the face of the teenage boy's informed and sensible statement.

Around this same time, when assigned to write a composition about how much good had been achieved for Italy with the seizure of the Papal States, Eugenio roundly condemned the move as plain robbery and persecution. He might well have been expelled from school for such anti-nationalist sentiments, but his teachers thought him too intelligent and talented to be dismissed.

Eugenio's education was strict and demanding. Records show that he was at the top of every class he attended, and he graduated with highest honors. His memory was phenomenal, not just in Italian but in any one of the many languages at his command. He had no difficulty learning Latin. He possessed what today would be called a photographic memory—the ability to comprehend and retain pages of any book he read with great rapidity.

Pacelli had many hobbies. He was a natural for dramatics. His teachers recognized his ability to speak and captivate an audience. Summers were spent at the family home in Onano, where he liked to ride his horse. He was also a good swimmer in Lake Bolsena, and he was swift and tireless as a canoeist. As a hiker he had the reputation of being unbeatable. His collection of coins and stamps was admired by his friends. From an early age he maintained an ardent interest in archaeology, and carefully researched and studied inscriptions of early Christians in the Catacombs.

A Break with Tradition

After a four-day retreat, Pacelli announced to his family that he would not follow family tradition and become a lawyer but that he intended to become a priest.

The announcement came as no surprise. The Pacellis knew that Eugenio had always been a serious, deeply committed and religious young boy and teenager. In 1894, at the age of eighteen, he entered the Capranica Seminary and enrolled at the Gregorian University. Not by nature physically robust, he taxed his body with prodigious study and prayers. At an early age he was afflicted with stomach difficulties that never disappeared, and early on there were signs of tuberculosis. For these reasons, thanks to Pope Leo XIII, who came to his rescue, Eugenio was given permission to live at home while he continued his courses at the Sapienza School of Philosophy and Letters as well as at the Papal Athenaum of St. Apollinaris for Theology. This was an unprecedented dispensation. He progressed rapidly through his studies and received his Baccalaureate and Licentiate degrees summa cum laude. His frail health prevented his participation at the graduation ceremony. He was ordained a priest on Easter Sunday, April 2, 1899, in Bishop Francesco Paolo Cassetta's private chapel. The next day, Eugenio Pacelli celebrated his first Mass in the Borghese Chapel of the Basilica of Saint Mary Major, in Rome.

Eugenio Pacelli was ordained a priest on April 2, 1899.

As a boy, Eugenio loved to play the violin. He was exceptionally talented, and often the entire family enjoyed listening while he played and his sisters accompanied him on the mandolin. As a young priest he would, whenever his pressing studies and duties allowed, refresh his soul by playing the violin. It was during one of these occasions that the then Monsignor Pietro Gasparri came to give him some very important news. He told him that the Vatican was impressed with his abilities and wanted him to take an apprentice position in the Vatican's Secretariat of State. Pacelli lowered his violin and said: "But I had hoped to spend my life as a shepherd of souls." At the time, little did Father Pacelli know that he was destined to be the Church's supreme shepherd of souls.

CHAPTER II

Priestly Career

Father Eugenio Pacelli's first assignment was as a parish priest at Chiesa Nuova, the church where he had served as an altar boy. While there, he taught catechism to the children, who loved him because he was gentle, kind, patient, and understanding. At the same time he pursued his studies for a doctorate in Canon Law and Civil Law at the Apollinaris. Incredibly, only two years later, he would add doctorates in Philosophy and in Theology.

An indication of the esteem in which young Pacelli was held by the leaders of the Church at the end of the nineteenth and the beginning of the twentieth century is the fact that he was selected for a very delicate diplomatic mission in 1901. In that year Queen Victoria died, and Pope Leo XIII sent Father Pacelli to London with a personal handwritten letter of condolence for her son, King Edward VII.

In 1904, Father Pacelli became a Papal Chamberlain with the title of Monsignor and one year later a Domestic Prelate. The reception of all these honors did not keep the new Monsignor from continuing to teach catechism to children in one of Rome's poorest quarters or from conducting spiritual conferences for the French Sisters of Namur who ran an academy for girls of the Roman aristocracy. All this time he counseled in spiritual matters working girls who resided at the House of Saint Rose.

His own spiritual life continued to be intense and exemplary. Furthermore, in addition to morning meditation and Mass, Pacelli always managed to find two hours a day to spend on his knees before the Blessed Sacrament. It would be a pattern he would follow his entire life.

Pacelli was again sent to England in 1908, where he attended the Eucharistic Congress in London. The thirty-two-year-old priest was by that time well embarked on what would become a nearly forty-year career of brilliant diplomatic service for the Church. From 1904 to 1916, he was a research aide in the Office of the Congregation of Extraordinary Ecclesiastical Affairs, where he assisted Cardinal Pietro Gasparri in the crucial task of clarifying and updating canon law.

In 1910, Monsignor Pacelli was again back in London, where he represented the Holy See at the coronation of King George V. This trip demonstrated some remarkable ingenuity on the gifted priest's part. While unpacking, he discovered that a bottle of iodine in his toilet kit had spilled on the pope's salutation to the new monarch. Pacelli made the best of what must have seemed a disastrous accident. He calmly swabbed more iodine over the entire document before presenting it to the king. It seemed to the monarch and to all who looked at the document as though it had been written on extremely ancient papal parchment.

In 1911, Pius X appointed Pacelli Undersecretary for Extraordinary Ecclesiastical Affairs. This department of the Secretariat of State negotiated terms of agreements with foreign governments that would allow the Church to carry out its teaching mission. In 1912, he was appointed Pro-Secretary. Two years later, he became Secretary of the Congregation of Extraordinary Ecclesiastical Affairs.

Difficulties in Germany

In 1914, Pius X died and Benedict XV was called to the Chair of Peter. On April 20, 1917, the new Pope appointed Monsignor Pacelli as Nuncio to Bavaria, Germany, a nation on the verge of military defeat and revolutionary

Pacelli was Archbishop of the titular See of Sardi. He presented Benedict XV's peace proposals to the Kaiser and dedicated himself to the assistance of prisoners of war.

chaos. Before assuming full responsibilities in Germany, Pacelli was consecrated a Bishop by Pope Benedict XV in the Sistine Chapel (May 13, 1917). Present were Pacelli's mother, father, brother and sisters, and five Cardinals. He was then elevated to the rank of Archbishop and went to Germany to present his credentials to Ludwig III, King of Bavaria, on May 28, 1917.

When he visited Kaiser Wilhelm II, Archbishop Pacelli begged him to do all in his power to end World War I. In his diary the Prussian wrote that he "liked the man from Rome well enough as a human being. But this was war. Let the British and French answer for it." Benedict XV's proposals for peaceful settlement were not accepted.

The Kaiser, unfortunately, thought that the collapse of the Russian army meant that the Germans could now concentrate on the French and British and quickly achieve victory. He had not calculated the impact of America's entering the war. As World War I continued on all fronts with renewed fury, the young Nuncio dedicated himself to tending to the spiritual and physical assistance of the sick and wounded men in hospitals and to assisting prisoners of war in their camps and in their attempts to communicate with their families. He was held in high esteem by both civil and ecclesiastical authorities. President von Hindenburg of Germany wrote of "the noble conception Archbishop Pacelli had of his office, his wise objectivity, his inflexible sense of justice, his generous humanity, and his great love for his neighbor."

American newspaper and radio commentator Dorothy Thompson wrote: "Those of us who were foreign correspondents in Berlin during the days of the Weimar Republic were not unfamiliar with the figure of the dean of the diplomatic corps: Tall, slender, with magnificent eyes, strong features and expressive hands, in his appearance and bearing....In knowledge of German and European affairs and in diplomatic astuteness the Nuncio was without an equal."

After the war, the papacy turned the attention of the allied powers to the great dangers that would arise "unless a peace which

Nuncio Pacelli distributes packages to prisoners of war in Germany during World War I.

Germans can accept and which is not humiliating for them…is reached." Most Germans found it difficult to live with the Treaty of Versailles of 1919, which, if not accepted, the Allies stated, would mean the resumption of their military operations.

An incident demonstrating Pacelli's support for a democratic-republican government took place in Munich in 1922. At a hostile political meeting, Konrad Adenauer, who later became Chancellor of the West German Republic, defended republicanism as the best hope for Germany. When Adenauer finished his speech, only Cardinal Pacelli, still the Papal Nuncio, clapped his hands enthusiastically. This was to be a preview of his support for democracy rooted in the laws of God as he explained in his 1944 Christmas address, and later demonstrated by encouraging the Christian Democrats in Italy after World War II.

Regardless of his private convictions, Pacelli saw republicanism as good for Germany. Therefore, when Cardinal Michael von Faulhaber rose for a rebuttal of Adenauer's arguments, Pacelli jerked at Faulhaber's cassock. The Cardinal was surprised, but he sat down and went along with the diplomatic intuitions of the Papal Nuncio.

Only Weapon: The Cross

After some time in Munich, the Apostolic Nuncio's residence was transferred to Berlin. His peace efforts did not succeed. The Germans were not ready for peace. As Nuncio and then as Vatican Secretary of State, Pacelli faced and feared the rise of the National Socialists.

With the defeat of Germany, Communist mobs seized control of Munich in February 1919. Every diplomat returned to safety, except Pacelli, who continued his errands of mercy toward the desperate public, overseeing the distribution of relief packages. To counter this work of mercy, the Bolsheviks instigated a campaign of hate against him. There was street rioting, and the socialist revolutionaries broke into Archbishop Pacelli's home. Armed terrorists had been ordered to storm the nunciature. With guns blazing they jumped through windows to confront him. Grenades shattered windows across his desk. They demanded that he surrender his car.

Tall and defiant, he slowly descended the stairs, stating: "You must leave at once! This house does not belong to the government, but to the Holy See. It is inviolable under international law." As he held his pectoral cross, the socialist leader stepped forward, jamming his gun against the Archbishop's chest. But the gun muzzle glanced off the pectoral cross, and seeing what he had struck, the man wavered and disappeared. Years later during a TV program, Bishop Fulton Sheen told his audience: "The cross Pacelli wore that day is the cross that I am wearing now!" He had received it as a token of the Pope's esteem.

A few days later, after delivering food and medical supplies to a center for children dying of starvation, another mob attacked Pacelli's car. The Nuncio ordered the chauffeur to stop the car and put down the top. While holding the cross high above his head for all to see, he blessed the mob. "My mission is peace," he said. "The only weapon we have is this cross....Why should you harm us?" Slowly, the crowd dispersed.

CHAPTER III

Anti-Semitic Persecution

The Lateran Treaty of 1929 established formal relations between Italy and the Vatican. Following the example of Mussolini, Adolf Hitler initiated a concordat. This is a strictly defined legal agreement between two governments intended to preserve the freedom of the Church to teach and minister to the faithful. Historically the Holy See has signed many such agreements. There was nothing unique about concordats with Italy in 1929 or with Germany in 1933. In fact, Pacelli negotiated a concordat with Bavaria which was signed on March 29, 1924, and concluded one with Prussia on June 14, 1929. Pacelli was then recalled to Rome and on December 16 received a Cardinal's hat. Soon after, on February 7, 1930, he was appointed Secretary of State (succeeding his former mentor Cardinal Pietro Gasparri) and became Archpriest of St. Peter's Basilica.

Cardinal Pacelli is named Archpriest of St. Peter's Basilica.

Cardinal Pacelli negotiated with the Germans to protect the rights of Catholics. The Holy See agreed especially since the new German regime was determined to tamper with the existing concordats with Bavaria and Prussia.

As long as the German government guaranteed freedom of religion, the Catholic Church, which was opposed to Nazi ideology, could express its point of view. However, the Holy See had to make concessions. Only party members were allowed to engage in politics. The Catholic clergy could no longer participate. Soon after, the official Protestant Church came under Nazi influence and a *Reichsbischof* was appointed.

The National Socialist Party exploited all the problems and fears of Germans to its own purpose, promising to achieve national unity, to undo the "shame" of Versailles, and to make Germany great again. The party vowed to fight Communism and any form of Marxism.

President Paul von Hindenburg, who for many years had refused to appoint Adolf Hitler as Chancellor, succumbed to the opposition on January 30, 1933. In replacing Franz von Papen, a former Catholic Center Party member, Hitler became the leader of the largest party in the Reichstag.

Jewish descendants, even if baptized, were deprived of their German citizenship. In 1934, after *Kristallnacht*, the infamous "Night of the Long Knives," when the Nazis initiated their first large-scale massacre, Cardinal Pacelli had the Vatican newspaper unequivocally condemn the Nazi crimes.

"The *Osservatore*," wrote French correspondent Charles Pichon, "in three articles, proclaimed that National Socialism better deserved the name of 'national terrorism,' and that like all movements which resort to terrorism, it sprang from a gang rather than from a party."[1]

The Nazi government now engaged in open warfare against the Church. In fact, Hitler's principal collaborator, Martin Bormann, declared: "We Germans are the first to be appointed by destiny to break with Christianity. It will be an honor for us. A thousand ties link us to the Christian faith; they will be broken with a single blow. Our intention is not to raze the cathedrals to the ground, but to fill them with a new ideology and with proclamations of a new faith."[2]

In 1935, Cardinal Pacelli was the Papal Legate to Lourdes to officiate at the closing celebrations of the Holy Year.

In a letter dated March 12, 1935, to Cardinal Schulte of Cologne, Pacelli attacked the Nazis as "false prophets with the pride of Lucifer," labeling them "bearers of a new faith and a new gospel" who were attempting to create a "mendacious antinomy between faithfulness to the Church and to the Fatherland."[3]

The following month, Cardinal Pacelli delivered an address before a quarter of a million people at Lourdes, April 25–28, 1935, where he described the Nazis as "possessed by the superstition of race and blood" and declared that "the Church does not consent to form a compact with them at any price." Describing the speech, the *New York Times* headlined its story: "Nazis Warned at Lourdes" (April 29, 1935).

Visit to the United States of America

Cardinal Pacelli represented Pope Pius XI on many occasions. He was sent to Buenos Aires, Argentina, aboard the *Conte Grande* and presided as Papal Legate at the International Eucharistic Congress, October 10–14, 1934. He was also Pope Pius XI's delegate to France for the closing days of the Jubilee Year honoring the nineteenth centenary of Redemption. In 1936 he visited the United States of America.

Planes accompanied the *Conte di Savoia*, October 8, 1936, as the ship sailed down New York Harbor and passed the Statue of Liberty. Cardinal Eugenio Pacelli was a Vatican representative. During the official salute, fireboats sprayed the harbor with multicolored streams; warships fired volley after volley high into the sky; sailboats, steamers, yachts, barges, rowboats proudly showed the papal colors of yellow and white.

Upon his arrival in New York, Cardinal Pacelli was met by over fifty journalists and photographers. Pacelli stated: "I am indeed happy to find myself within the territory of a great people who know how to unite so beautifully and so nobly a sense of discipline and the exercise of a just, legitimate and well-ordered liberty." Smiling happily, he walked down the gangway determined to see America as a tourist.

The trip was billed as a vacation for Cardinal Pacelli, but reporters felt the Vatican Secretary of State came to silence the radio priest, Father Charles E. Coughlin, and take the Catholic Church out of the American presidential campaign.

Pacelli made contact with every aspect of American life. His first stop was to St. Patrick's Cathedral in Manhattan and the residence of Patrick Cardinal Hayes. There he lunched with Nicholas Murray Butler, President of Columbia University. He visited the Empire State Building and admired the skyline of New York, and in Philadelphia he saw the Liberty Bell. He had a whirlwind

Cardinal Pacelli visits the Cathedral of St. Paul, Minnesota. To his right is Archbishop John Gregory Murray.

17

tour of the United States: Cleveland, Chicago, Notre Dame, San Francisco, Boulder Dam, Minneapolis, Kansas City, and Notre Dame University, where he was awarded an honorary L.L.D.

The children of Sacred Heart School in Massachusetts presented a special program in his honor. Cardinal Pacelli congratulated them in English, concluding with "I wish to tell you that I thoroughly enjoyed it. I realize that you must have worked very hard. And therefore I grant you two holidays, today and tomorrow." Remembering his own school days, he accepted the thunderous applause as gratitude for the free days rather than tribute to himself.

Among other stops he visited Richard Cardinal Cushing in Boston and the Knights of Columbus headquarters in New Haven, Connecticut. On October 21 he went to Baltimore and was welcomed by Archbishop Michael Curley as he visited the Cathedral of the Assumption and St. Mary's Seminary, both the oldest in the United States. The following day he went to Washington, D.C., and made the following stops: the Catholic University, the National Catholic Welfare

Cardinal Pacelli visits the Library of Congress, Washington D.C., and admires the Gutenberg Bible. Alongside the Cardinal is the librarian, Herbert Putnam.

Conference, and Georgetown University, where he received the honorary degree of doctor of canon and civil law. At the Library of Congress, he was interested in seeing the Declaration of Independence, the Constitution, and an original score of Abbé Franz Liszt, the Hungarian pianist and composer. He signed the guest register "E. Card. Pacelli." That same day he visited Mount

Cardinal Pacelli visits the Catholic University, Washington, D.C. He is greeted by Father Roth, O.P.

Vernon, the home and tombs of George and Martha Washington, where he placed memorial wreaths.

Fordham University

On Sunday afternoon, November 1, 1936, Fordham University held a special convocation in honor of His Eminence Eugenio Cardinal Pacelli, Secretary of State to His Holiness Pope Pius XI. With the University Band leading the procession from Keating Hall, the entire R.O.T.C. Unit marched past His Eminence, in column formation, to form a guard of honor. To welcome Cardinal Pacelli, a man in uniform stood on each side of the pathway, every five feet, all the way to the Gymnasium, where over five thousand guests were seated. Church dignitaries and distinguished guests followed in procession. Cameras and sound equipment recorded the proceedings. The Columbia network carried the Cardinal's voice on a coast-to-coast hookup, and millions of people throughout the country were able to see and hear the memorable ceremony. The Fordham University Glee Club presented a magnificent performance.

Addressing the audience, President Robert I. Gannon, S.J., made reference to the fact that the name Pacelli suggests peace; that the motto on his crest—*opus justitiae pax*—was indeed meaningful; that it is in the universities where the love of justice flourishes.

After his gracious acceptance of the honorary degree, Cardinal Pacelli spoke about the need for "an education that rests upon the rock of truth and not upon the sand of mere materialism, a truly Christian education illumined by the light of faith....Be true to the traditions of your Alma Mater and be not drawn away from those time-honored studies which have made saints and scholars in the Old World, and in the New World have produced leaders of men, loyal to God and to country, the strongest bulwark of the nation." The applause was enthusiastic!

Cardinal Pacelli then faced the student body to grant the customary day off. With a radiant smile, he announced: "I grant you a holi-day." The word he pronounced with a slight Italian accent sounded like "holy day." There was no reaction from the students and no one applauded. The silence alarmed the Cardinal, so he waved his hands in the air, shouting: "Free day!" "Free day!" This time his message sounded like "three days." The applause was deafening! The faux pas was later straightened out, but it was never forgotten.

Return to the Vatican

His trip to the United Sates was highly successful. This was an "unofficial" trip covering some eight thousand miles in seven days. Americans were awed into silence by his presence. He welcomed everyone, and thousands were able to greet him as he traveled across the country. The Vatican Secretary of State made an in-depth study of the American Church. He also appealed to the United States to throw open its doors to Jewish refugees, but his request went unheeded. On November 5, 1936, the eve of his return to the Vatican, President Franklin D. Roosevelt—who two days earlier had a landslide victory for a second term—invited Cardinal Pacelli to a luncheon at his home in Hyde Park, New York, where he was given a warm reception.

Joined by representatives of the clergy and laity, Cardinal Pacelli crossed Manhattan to board the ship at Pier 59 on the North River for his return voyage. In his written statement to the press he included the prayer "that Almighty God may continue to bless this great nation, that its citizens may be happy and prosperous and that the influence of the United States may always be exerted for the promotion of peace among peoples." As the color guard dipped the flags of the United States and the Holy See, the *Conte di Savoia* moved out into the river. It reached Naples on November 14. The Cardinal took a train for Rome, motored to Vatican City, and met for two hours with Pope Pius XI, giving him a detailed report on his journey.

Papal Encyclical

In his encyclical *Mit brennender Sorge*, prepared under the direction of Cardinal Pacelli, then Secretary of State, Pope Pius XI condemned anti-Semitism. The encyclical, written in German for wider dissemination in that country, was smuggled out of Italy, copied, and distributed to parish priests to be read from all of the pulpits on Palm Sunday, March 14, 1937. It was immediately confiscated, printers were arrested, and presses seized. The following day *Das Schwarze Korps* called it "the most incredible of Pius XI's pastoral letters: every sentence in it was an insult to the new Germany."

Cardinal Pacelli returned to France in 1937, as Cardinal-Legate to consecrate and dedicate the new basilica in Lisieux during the Eucharistic Congress and made another anti-Nazi statement. He again presided on May 25–30, 1938, at the International Eucharistic Congress in Budapest.

CHAPTER IV

Election of Pope Pius XII

On February 28, 1939, the *New York Times* reported: "The Jewish issue in Italy is growing more intense and is one of the gravest of the many serious problems being considered by the Cardinals who will enter the conclave...to elect a new Pope."[4]

The Cardinals elected Eugenio Pacelli—the 262nd Pope—on his sixty-third birthday, March 2, 1939. He received sixty-one out of the sixty-two votes (all but his own) and was elected Pontiff. He selected the name of his predecessor Pius XI and became Pope Pius XII. The bells of Saint Peter's pealed on March 12, 1939, the day of his coronation, as the eyes of a million people turned toward the balcony where Pius XII was dressed in a white cope and wearing a silver, gem-studded mitre on his head.

Cardinal Nicola Canali removes the mitre. Cardinal Camillo Caccia-Dominioni replaces it with the papal tiara.

After his coronation, the voice of Pius XII rings out across St. Peter's Square in a blessing on the city and on the world.

Pope Pius XII's coat-of-arms showed the symbol of peace: a dove with an olive branch. His motto indicated peace to be a fruit of justice: *Opus justitiae pax* (Is. 34, 17). His first radio message to the world was, "Peace, gift of God, desired by all upright men, the fruit of love and justice." He was a man of peace.

Immediately after his election, Pius XII issued a call for a peace conference of European leaders. Documents show that in a last-minute bid to avert bloodshed, the Pope called for a conference involving Italy, France, England, Germany, and Poland. Pius XII's peace plan was based on five points: the defense of small nations, the right to life, disarmament, some new kind of League of Nations, and a plea for the moral principles of justice and love. Through his public discourses, his appeals to governments, and his secret diplomacy, he was engaged more than any other individual in the effort to avert war and rebuild peace. His request went unheeded.

Pius XII then met with the German Cardinals who had been present in the recent conclave, in order to ascertain the real situation of the Church in Nazi Germany. These meetings provided him with direct proof and information that motivated the content of his first encyclical, *Summi Pontificatus*.

Dated October 20, 1939, this encyclical was a strong attack on totalitarianism. In it, Pius XII singled out those governments that by their deification of the state imperiled the spirit of humanity. He spoke about restoring the foundation of human society to its origin in natural law, to its source in Christ, the only true ruler of all men and women of all nations and races. Indeed, Pius XII's encyclicals, discourses, and radio messages clearly assert that the only solid foundation for social order is the law of God.

World War II

The Catholic Church is not a political institution but a spiritual one whose mission is to obtain the eternal salvation of all men, of every race and country. For this reason, the traditional policy of the Church in time of war is neutrality. It cannot ally itself with or against any nation or nations. It must tell the nations of the world what Christian morality permits and forbids; it must condemn crimes against justice and charity; it must ease the sufferings of the war's victims. Although neutral as to the political aspects of war, the Church is belligerent as to its moral aspects.

On the eve of World War II, the international position of the Vatican was dangerous and difficult. The anti-Semitic decrees enacted by Mussolini in 1938 were causing bitter conflicts between Italy and the Holy See.

As a diplomat, Pius XII saw war approaching and instructed the papal representatives to Germany, Italy, France, Poland, and England to learn whether mediation by the Pope would be considered. On August 24, 1939, he gave each papal representative the text of a speech asking them to convey it to their respective governments. That evening he read the speech to the world: "The danger is imminent, but there is still time. Nothing is lost with peace; all can be lost with war."

Requests for information were received from every country in the world.

Without interruption before and during the war, Pius XII continued his work for peace, striving to heal the wounds inflicted by this great tragedy. The papacy rescued Jews by channeling money to those in need, issuing countless baptismal certificates for their protection, negotiating with Latin American countries to grant them visas, and keeping in touch with their relatives through the Vatican Information Service.

During the North African campaign a boatload of Allied wounded arrived in Italy for hospitalization and imprisonment. A Vatican representative boarded the boat and distributed message forms among the soldiers, who immediately filled, signed, and addressed them. Within weeks after their capture, the families of these American soldiers received information sent airmail by the Vatican to the United States. A wounded son of an Episcopalian family in Washington, D.C., was listed by the War Department as missing, because the Nazis had failed to report him to the International Red Cross as captured. The soldier was convalescing in a hospital in Italy, where a Vatican official found him. A Baptist family in Kansas, as an expression of gratitude for news that their son was a war prisoner and not dead, sent the Holy Father their weekly tithe of twenty-two dollars. Communicating with their families, the Vatican described details of injuries, deaths, internment, and photographs of the resting-place or turned over to the office of the American chargé d'affaires the belongings of soldiers. This was a sad yet consoling work of mercy.

In view of the plight of the Jewish people of Europe, resolutions were adopted at the January 1939 meeting of the Jewish Congress in Geneva. Dr. Nahum Goldmann, chairman, stated: "We record the Jewish people's deep appreciation of the stand taken by the Vatican against the advance of resurgent paganism which challenges all traditional values of religion as well as inalienable human rights upon which alone enduring civilization can be found."[5]

On September 1, 1939, Nazi tanks crossed the Polish border. This was the beginning of World War II. In his encyclical *Summi Pontificatus* (October 27, 1939), Pius XII condemned Hitler's actions. On December 28, 1939, the Pope paid a ceremonial call on King Victor Emmanuel III and Queen Elena at the Quirinal Palace. The visit was to return that made by the King and Queen a week earlier and also to demonstrate the Vatican's support of Italy's neutrality.

Refugees, mostly women and children, make a home in the papal apartments at Castelgandolfo.

Historical records show that Pius XII acted as a link to the British government for a number of German dissidents desiring to overthrow Hitler. The Pope went beyond his usual caution and maintained these contacts until the German invasion of Denmark and Norway in April 1940. The following month, when the Germans invaded the Low Countries, the Pope sent telegrams to the leaders of these besieged nations with his prayers for their deliverance. Soon after, Mussolini joined Hitler. When Nazis occupied Rome in September 1943, the Pope endeavored to save as many Jews as possible. He immediately issued directives to all convents and monasteries to open their doors to protect Jews. Meanwhile, Pope Pius XII invited Jews and other refugees to join the Vatican Palatine Guards. In a few months, their number increased from four hundred to four thousand.

Everywhere in Europe, persecuted people, the Jews especially, appealed to Pius XII. When some five hundred Jews embarked at Bratislava on a steamer for Palestine, their ship tried to enter the seaport of Istanbul but was refused permission to land. Captured by an Italian patrol boat, the Jews were imprisoned in a camp at Rhodes. One of the prisoners managed to appeal to Pius XII for help. Thanks to the Pope's intervention, unknown to the Axis, the refugees were transferred to an improvised camp (Ferramonti-Tarsia) in southern Italy, where they were found safe three years later, in December 1943.[6]

CHAPTER V

Papal Audiences

For almost two decades, from March 2, 1939, to his death on October 9, 1958, Pius XII was entrusted with the keys of supreme jurisdiction given to the Prince of the Apostles: "Thou art Peter and upon this rock I will build My Church."

During World War II, people crowded around Pius XII. He received hundreds of thousands of servicemen and servicewomen of every Allied nation. One audience inspired American sailors to begin a rousing "Hip, hip, hooray—His Holiness!" Totally exhausted after the audiences, the Pope was always exhilarated by the expressions of love and respect of thousands of his flock from every part of the world. The overwhelming enthusiasm reflects the almost universal esteem for Pius XII and the belief that the Pope is, in fact, the representative of Christ on earth.

Pope Pius XII greets sailors.

Young girls from different parts of the world present gifts to the Holy Father on his birthday.

The Pope always enjoyed receiving people of every nation and rank: statesmen and workers; writers and artists; the young and the old; the sick and the suffering; religious and lay men and women. Offering their gifts, young people opened their hearts and confided to him their cherished dreams. As a father with his children, he spoke to them according to their particular state, profession, work, or condition.

Whether it was privately or in small or large groups, each person visiting His Holiness was truly a guest during a papal audience. No matter where one was staying in Rome, whenever invitations were requested, they were delivered by hand.

Everyone was his guest. Pope Pius XII called the audiences "windows on the world." This daily experience was kaleidoscopic and sometimes a source of confusion: pieces of clothing were lost, his hands bruised, and his pectoral cross broken. His movements were quick. One day he was not aware that his ring slipped off his hand. As a woman knelt earlier to kiss it, the ring remained in her hand. The elderly woman screamed that she had to see the Pope.

The guards wanted to arrest her, but the Pope smilingly told her to approach him and then asked her to slip his "fisherman's" ring back on.

Each morning, following Pius XII's meetings with Vatican staff members, he had private or general audiences for people in all walks of life. Addressing each group, he reminded them of their duties and obligations and had extraordinary insight into all types of problems.

To bankers the Pope cautioned that money is not an end in itself but merely an instrument to be used justly for securing the God-given rights of all men. To midwives he clarified the Church's continued stand against abortion and contraceptive practices. He recalled that this is not just Catholic teaching. It is rooted in the natural law, the rules of Creation as God made the world. He not only showed his appreciation of good craftsmanship as he spoke to jewelers but told streetcar conductors that he understood their vexations on the job. They knew he was trying to teach them the virtue of patience.

Pius XII loved sports. Athletes in every sport were warmly received. Far from causing them to be timid in his presence, he

His Holiness congratulates Gino Bartali, champion of the 1948 Tour de France.

would question them about
their particular sport and
manifest a vivid interest in
their latest developments. He
would often recall his visit to
the United States during the
1936 World Series between
the New York Yankees and the
Giants. To athletes he said
that the important thing
about sports is that it develops
willpower and Christian dom-
ination of the body as well as
"elevates the spirit above
small-mindedness, dishonesty,
and trickery."

Pius XII welcomes doctors at an international meeting.

Throughout his life Pacelli would find time for scholarly pur-
suits. In 1943, for example, in a discourse to the Pontifical Academy
of Science, he forecast the development of atomic energy and dis-
cussed the disintegration which uranium undergoes when bom-
barded by neutrons. The Pope expressed the hope that its force
would be harnessed for the service of man and not released for his
destruction.

On September 19, 1945, the *New York Times* wrote: "Pope
Pius XII this morning received Sir Alexander Fleming and dis-
cussed with him new uses of penicillin. The discoverer of penicillin
presented the Pope a plate for cultivating mold to be used in
research. Sir Alexander, after a twenty-minute audience, declared
he was astonished at the Pope's knowledge of his discovery."

In 1951 Pius XII spoke on modern science and the proofs for
the existence of God. On another occasion, he addressed the
International Astronomical Union and spoke on the histopathology
of the central nervous system. His speeches ranged from international penal law, toleration, psychiatry, and clinical psychology to
medical genetics, ophthalmology, urology, medico-moral problems,

> How exalted, how worthy of all honour is the character of your profession!
> The doctor has been appointed by God Himself (cf. Eccli. 38,1) to minister to the needs of suffering
> humanity. He who created that fever-consumed or mangled frame, now in
> your hands, who loves it with an eternal love, confides to you the ennobling
> charge of restoring it to health. You will bring to the sick-room and the operating
> table something of the charity of God, of the love and tenderness of Christ,
> the Master Physician of soul and body.
>
> That the blessing of the King of Kings may descend upon you and
> your work and all your dear ones and your beloved country and remain forever, is the wish
> and prayer that rise from Our affectionate heart.

Extract in English of his discourse to the doctors in his own handwriting.

as well as accountancy and economics, moral guidance, and statistics. Most of them were in French and Italian, but a few were in Spanish, German, English, or Latin.

Vatican Protocol

Pius XII blended informality with dignity and many times ignored Vatican protocol during the papal audiences. On some occasions, people filled with repentance would tremblingly ask to go to confession. Always a priest and aware of divine grace at work, the Holy Father never failed to step to a corner with the penitent sinner and grant him absolution while others waited in awe.

In those days, women admitted to a papal audience had to wear long-sleeved, high-necked black dresses with a mantilla and a veil. A young woman newspaper correspondent during World War II was in a hurry, so her male companions smuggled her past guards to the great Consistorial Hall where the Pope would receive them. But when instructed to form a circle, the conspirators were forced to expose the young lady. As the guards were rushing her away, the Pope entered and signaled them to let her stay. He repaid her brashness with the gentle comment: "Ah, we see you are an American."

Pius XII enjoys his visitors during a general audience.

Screening for a general audience was not very intense. In fact, many ladies were not aware they had to dress according to protocol. One day, when asked to kneel, a young girl in culottes and wedgies and harlequin glasses refused. "I got a coat on—isn't that enough? I'm not a Catholic! Why should I kneel?" Everyone was embarrassed.

As the Pope arrived, the girl continued to abuse the guards. Suddenly the scene changed. The Pope approached her gently; she burst into tears on her knees. He comforted her and stretched forth his hands to raise her up, but she shook her head and begged his blessing. Pope Pius XII blessed her and the rest of the assemblage.

A Man with a Sense of Compassion

Pius XII's love was manifested by his compassion. With thousands of people in larger audiences, the Pope had to move swiftly. One day there was a woman with a blind baby. He spoke consoling words to the woman while blessing her and the baby.

After moving away, Pius XII hesitated and then turned back. The Pope took the baby in his arms, pressed it tenderly to his heart, carefully protecting the child against his large, pectoral cross. He spoke quietly to the mother. The woman was weeping. So was Pius XII.

Pius XII's love was evident in his smiling, affectionate gaze. All who came to the audiences were well aware of his warmth. Regardless of one's faith, people in all walks of life and of every religious denomination treasured a meeting with him.

One day an American actor and his wife were present. As the Pope entered the room, he approached the newlyweds. They recall that "there was electricity in the room when he blessed them." They wished him a happy birthday. His smile lit up the whole room. The Pope gave them medals they would always treasure. "But," said the American actor, "it is Pius XII's simplicity and holiness which will stay with us forever to remind us that it's easy to reach God. He is only a prayer away."

On another occasion, the chamberlain called a family of Americans who were waiting for an audience—father, mother, and four children, the youngest in his mother's arms. When the baby began to cry, the mother pleaded with the chamberlain. He shook his head.

The mother saw a young woman and ran toward her. "Will you hold my baby for me?" she asked, and the surprised woman took him in her arms. However, soon the mother came hurrying back. "Thank you," she said. "Let me have my baby. His Holiness says he doesn't care if he cries. He wants to see him!"

Buried in the large group of faithful during a general audience, a soldier shifted uneasily on his crutches. He could not kneel. Suddenly he saw Pius XII's compassionate eyes looking at him. Walking toward him, the Pope extended his hand. The soldier fumbled his hat from his right hand to his left in order to grasp the Pope's, and he dropped it.

His Holiness bent down, grabbed the hat, placed it in the soldier's trembling hand, and embraced him. The young man suddenly relaxed and smiled. As the Pope moved on, the soldier leaned on his crutches, held his hat aloft in triumph, and then joined the crowd shouting, *Viva il Papa! Viva il Papa!*

A Man with a Sense of Humor

During one papal audience, a group of American baseball players were amazed when Pius XII spoke about sports. One of them waited till the audience was almost over, and as the Pope turned away, he murmured, "I was a Cardinal once myself, Your Holiness." Immediately the Pope turned around: "And how could that have been, my son?" During the explanation, a perplexed Pius XII grinned. The baseball player treasures the Pope's reaction: "I guess I really walked into that one." Joe Medwick, of the Saint Louis Cardinals, could never figure out where he got the nerve to kid the Pope.

On another occasion, an Anglican lady was invited to a special audience. She was alone and awaited the Pope in a small chamber. Now and then people dressed in the oddest fashions (e.g., the Swiss Guards in an outfit designed by Michelangelo and others in long robes) reassured her that the Pope would soon arrive. A tall, thin man wearing a white cassock chatted with her. She responded to his gentle questioning and they had a few polite laughs.

At one point the Anglican lady whispered: "Confidentially, the main reason I want to see the Pope is because a lot of my Catholic friends gave me rosaries and medals and Lord knows what else for him to bless."

"We shall be happy to do so," said the man in white. The lady's jaw dropped. "Oh, no," she gulped. "You're the Pope!"

In 1950, the Pope welcomed the American comedians Olsen and Johnson to the Vatican. "Laughter has no religion," Pius XII wistfully emphasized as he spoke about God's generosity with the gift of laughter. "There should be more of it in the world."

A few days after the liberation of Rome, Lieutenant General Mark Clark, Commander of the Fifth Allied Army, paid his respects to the Pope: "I am afraid you have been disturbed by the noise of my tanks. I am sorry." Pius XII smiled and replied: "General, any time you come to liberate Rome, you can make just as much noise as you like."

Robert Murphy, U.S. Undersecretary of State, and Pius XII were among the diplomats in Germany during the mid-1920s. When they met after the war, Murphy reminisced about how they had underestimated Hitler. Both had reported to their governments that he would never come to power. In response to Murphy, the Pope smiled and said, "In those days, you see, I was not infallible."

A Man with a Sense of Justice

Although Pius XII would not publicize his own good deeds, others have. It suffices to mention a recent story which is part of the official Italian war record (*International Herald Tribune*, October 22, 2001). This information is one of the many examples of Pius XII's actions on behalf of Jewish refugees:

From 1943 to 1945, Leonardo Marinelli was a commander in the Royal Finance Guard in the Aprica internment camp, located in northern Italy. His *Diary* records an entry for September 12, 1943. The Pope sent Giuseppe Carozzi, a young Italian priest, to Marinelli requesting that three hundred Jewish Yugoslav internees be given permits to Switzerland. Despite strict Nazi orders forbidding Jews, prisoners of war, or anyone who had not joined Mussolini's northern Italian puppet Republic of Salò from crossing the border, Marinelli complied with the Pope's wishes. During the next four days, as the group crossed the border, guards were seen "carrying bags for some of the fugitives."

Later, Marinelli himself was placed in an internment camp by the Nazis. He escaped. In his testimony to the Finance Guard high command in July 1945, Marinelli confirmed what he had written in his *Diary*.

Pius XII's personal magnetism, his warmth and affection, his compassion and love are characteristics that inspire everyone who has had the privilege of being in his presence. Each person was regarded as his personal guest. Though burdened with the cares of the world, Pius XII listened attentively to all who approached him. He radiated sanctity and peace; his dark, luminous eyes looked at everyone with paternal affection. Whenever someone requested his zucchetto, he would willingly give it. I have one in my possession. Indeed, I re-live those precious moments when, during the *baciamano* in Saint Peter's Basilica, his niece, Elena Rossignani Pacelli, introduced me to him in 1957.

Vatican Relief Efforts

Vatican relief efforts—clothes, food, medicine, books—for the suffering throughout the world stemmed from Pius XII. The ceasing of hostilities did not end the sufferings of homeless survivors. At Villa Walsh, Morristown, New Jersey, Mother Ninetta Jonata started a campaign in support of Pius XII's efforts and helped relieve the terrible destruction, hunger, sickness, and death caused by the brutal conflict. Countless cases of food, clothing, medicine, and other necessities were prepared at Villa Walsh and sent to the Pope for the relief of destitute war victims. The last shipload arrived in Naples on the

The Pope visits the Vatican bakery before distribution of bread to wartime victims.

37

Vatican trucks prepare for distribution of food to refugees in Rome.

Michelangelo (June 3, 1966) and was brought to the Vatican storehouse for distribution to the needy. It arrived on the Vatican railway (the world's shortest). The marble station, less than one-fifth of a mile of track from warehouse to outer wall, connected with the Italian state railroad. The Vatican enjoyed a freight discount of more than half on any shipment that entered the walls. Materials for mission and relief work were then transferred to a needy world.

A letter from the Secretary of State, dated June 18, 1947, refers to cases of supplies that had arrived within a few months from America: "29 cases on the ship, *City of Athens;* 60 cases on the *Exiria;* 90 cases on the *Waimea.*" This letter included a request for soccer balls to help children adjust in the aftermath of the war. In his own hand the Pope wrote: "Your generous charity, beloved daughter, towards the suffering poor of Italy has been brought to Our attention. It has helped Us to widen the field of Our benefactions...December 31, 1949, Pius pp. XII."

Pius XII took special care of Vatican personnel. Only Vatican City residents could buy at its supermarket at one-half the cost elsewhere. The farm at Castelgandolfo supplied much of the produce, eggs, cheese, and milk. During World War II there were four hundred New Hampshire chickens for eggs, and nearly fifty Frisian cows for milk. Much of what the farm provided was sent free to a hospital in Rome.

Vox Populi, Vox Dei!

Pius XII was the "Good Shepherd." He took care of his flock and remained in Rome during World War II. When Jews and other refugees were hidden in the Vatican, he provided for their needs. Whenever possible, kosher foods for the Jews were supplied. Because everyone else could not have heat during the winter months, he refused to have heat in his apartment. He would not accept coffee during the war when he could not serve it to his "guests."

In 1943, as millions of Jews and other Europeans suffered the horrors of the Holocaust, the eternal city was bombed during a two-hour attack. The Holy Father hurried from the Vatican to the streets of Rome. He stood in the midst of terrorized people as buildings collapsed in piles of smoldering rubble and bombs exploded on all sides. The Romans ran toward him for guidance and strength. With hands and white cassock smeared with the blood of the dead and the wounded, Pius XII blessed and consoled his flock. While civil authorities fled, the Pope personally took care

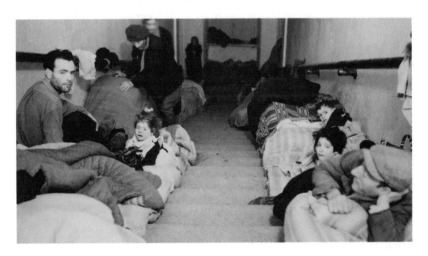

Homeless and refugees in makeshift dormitories at Castelgandolfo.

July 19, 1943—Pope Pius XII addressing the crowd after the bombing of Rome.

of the immediate needs of the victims, providing food and distributing funds to the homeless.

Pope Pius XII was the "Good Shepherd," selflessly dedicated to the Church and to the glory of God. Contrary to how posterity has portrayed him, he was truly interested in the lives of approximately 450,000,000 members of his flock and in all members of the human race.

The Romans gave him the title *Defensor Civitatis*; his contemporaries throughout the world acclaimed him *Pastor Angelicus*. Indeed, the voice of the people is the voice of God. *Vox populi, Vox Dei!*

CHAPTER VI

Campaign of Vilification

The Catholic Church did not surrender into silence. In fact, numerous protests and interventions were made through the nuncios and the ambassadors. When Adolf Hitler was nominated Chancellor of Germany on January 30, 1933, the first official step taken by the Vatican Secretary of State, Cardinal Eugenio Pacelli, who six years later would become Pope Pius XII, was to defend the Jews. Robert Leiber, S.J., clearly demonstrates that the Holy See informed the Apostolic Nunzio in Berlin to "officially represent the Vatican defense of the Jews with the German Government and to alert the Nazis about the dangers of anti-Semitic politics."

Truth and justice demand a re-evaluation of the attacks against Pius XII, claiming "silence," "moral culpability," or "anti-Semitism." *L'Osservatore Romano* condemned Adolf Hitler, Nazism, racism, and anti-Semitism by name. Cardinal Secretary of State Pacelli's efforts to prevent World War II and the Holocaust have been ignored. His messages on Vatican Radio, his participation in the plot of German generals to overthrow Hitler, the testimony of countless witnesses, Eichmann's diaries, the Pope's intervention for Lend-Lease to Russia, the evidence produced at Nuremberg, the extraordinary Jewish tributes, the hundreds of pages of sworn depositions—all are dismissed by his accusers.

Throughout his papacy, Pope Pius XII was almost universally regarded as a saintly man, a scholar, a man of peace, a tower of strength, and a compassionate defender of all victims of the war and genocide that had drenched Europe in blood. At the end of the war Western nations paid tribute to his efforts on behalf of the oppressed. When Pius XII died, Jews praised him for his help and were among the first to express sorrow and gratitude for his solicitude during the Holocaust.

Documentary evidence and the testimony of his contemporaries prove that Pius XII was a committed protector of the victims of war and hatred. Pius XII ordered the Congregation of the Holy Office to issue a formal and explicit condemnation of the mass murder going on in Germany in the name of improving the race. The decree was published on December 6, 1940, in *L'Osservatore Romano*. At the end of World War II, Western nations paid tribute to Pius XII's efforts on behalf of the oppressed. When he died in 1958, the Jewish communities of Europe praised him for his help and expressed sorrow and gratitude for his solicitude during the Holocaust. In the 1960s, there began a campaign of vilification against Pius XII. Today his detractors continue to claim that he lacked courage, human compassion, and a sense of moral rectitude. Hostile attacks by the media replace the historical record that showed him as a great leader.

This is the continuation of a smear campaign against the memory of Pius XII that began with Rolf Hochhuth's play, *The Deputy*, staged for the first time in 1963 in Germany. This "black legend," accusing the Pope of refusing to speak out about the Holocaust in spite of his detailed knowledge of Jewish suffering, was devoid of any fact.

If the Pope had openly condemned the Nazis, he would have also had to openly condemn the Fascists and the Communists. He was a prisoner of the Germans and of the Italians. Nazi and Fascist intelligence organizations invaded the Vatican. Important services were entirely controlled by the Italian government: food, water, electricity, sewage. Communication was censored: mail, telephone, and telegraph.

The Allies wanted Pius XII to condemn the Nazis, but they did not want him to criticize the Communists. Pius XII could not violate neutrality. Nor could he make partial public condemnations. Nonetheless, the Pope's voice was heard on the Vatican Radio and in *L'Osservatore Romano*.

The Record

Although the world had not listened in 1939 to his pleas for peace and justice, the Pope tried to help alleviate the suffering of thousands of victims. In fact, when American bombers dropped tons of explosives on Rome, July 19, 1943, Pius XII comforted the injured, administered the Last Rites, and distributed money to those in need of food and clothing.

During the two-hour bombardment, buildings collapsed and bombs exploded on all sides. Constantly solicitous for the flock entrusted to him, the Pope hurried from the Vatican to the damaged Basilica of Saint Lawrence Outside the Walls. The people of Rome regarded him as a man of peace and a defender and protector of all victims of the war. Documents reveal Pius XII's constant, untiring steps and appeals on behalf of peace before and during the war. His efforts can only be characterized as extraordinary.

The persecution of the Catholic Church by the Nazis was evidenced by the incarceration of priests, sisters, and brothers. Both Protestant and Catholic clergy in Holland sent an open letter about the treatment of Jews and other minorities to Arthur Seyss-Inquart, the Reich Commissar, who then threatened that, unless they were silent, he would round up baptized Jews. Catholic bishops refused to obey and, on July 20, 1942, sent a pastoral letter that was read from all Catholic pulpits in the Netherlands.

The National Socialist Mayor of Rotterdam responded: "When the terrorism of the Church widens its scope and calls for sabotage, as it did in these letters, the time has come for the party to react in an appropriate manner."[7] Consequently, Jewish converts to Catholicism, including Edith Stein, were rounded up and sent to the concentration camps; Jewish converts to Protestantism were left unharmed.

Information appeared in the Milan newspaper *Il Giornale*, July 5, 1998, confirming what some historians have always believed—Hitler intended to kidnap the Pope. In fact, Hitler gave orders to occupy the Vatican. However, his plans did not materialize.

Gratitude of the Jewish Community

On December 1, 1944, the *Times* reported that the World
Jewish Congress publicly thanked the Holy See for its protection of
Jews, especially in Hungary; in October 1945, the World Jewish
Congress made a financial gift to the Vatican in recognition of the
Vatican's work to save the Jews; in May 1955, the Israeli
Philharmonic gave a command performance of Beethoven's
Seventh Symphony at the Vatican as a gesture of thanks to the Pope
for his services to Jews during the war. Delighted with the magnif-
icent performance, the Pontiff was photographed in the midst of
the Israeli orchestra, gave his blessing, and afterward granted an
audience to the musicians.

In contrast to the esteem Pius XII enjoyed until his death in
1958, his reputation today suffers many unjust attacks. Some say
that a theological condemnation of the Holocaust would have made
a difference. Others want to weaken the moral authority of the
papacy. However, according to Michael Novak, these critics "are
deflecting attention from themselves....Today's charges against
Pope Pius XII cannot stand scrutiny."[8]

On May 26, 1955, the Israeli Philharmonic performed Beethoven's Seventh
Symphony in the presence of Pius XII in gratitude for having saved so many
Jews.

What Pius XII did for the Jews directly and indirectly through his diplomatic representatives and the bishops is well documented. At the end of World War II, Dr. Joseph Nathan, representing the Hebrew Commission, addressed the Jewish community, expressing heartfelt gratitude to those who protected and saved Jews during the Nazi-Fascist persecutions. "Above all," he stated, "we acknowledge the Supreme Pontiff and the religious men and women who, executing the directives of the Holy Father, recognized the persecuted as their brothers and, with great abnegation, hastened to help them, disregarding the terrible dangers to which they were exposed."

Reuben Resnick, American Director of the Committee to Help Jews in Italy, declared that "all the members of the Catholic hierarchy in Italy, from Cardinals to Priests, saved the lives of thousands of Jews, men, women, and children who were hosted and hidden in convents, churches, and other religious institutions."[9]

Chief Rabbi Alexander Safran, of Bucharest, Rumania, made the following statement on April 7, 1944, to Andrea Cassulo, Papal Nuncio to Rumania: "In the most difficult hours which we Jews of Rumania have passed through, the generous assistance of the Holy See was decisive and salutary."

The following petition was presented to Pope Pius

An article in a Geneva newspaper (September 8, 1942) tells how Pius XII protested the treatment of Jews in Vichy, France. The Pétain government had instructed local Church authorities to ignore the papal protest. Nevertheless, it was read in most churches.

XII in the summer of 1945 by twenty thousand Jewish refugees from Central Europe: "Allow us to ask the great honor of being able to thank, personally, His Holiness for the generosity he has shown us when we were being persecuted during the terrible period of Nazi-Fascism."

There was a story in an American newspaper (January 1946) about a special Thanksgiving service in Rome's Jewish Temple that was heard over the radio. The Jewish chaplain of the Fifth American Army said: "If it had not been for the truly substantial assistance and the help given to Jews by the Vatican and by Rome's ecclesiastical authorities, hundreds of refugees and thousands of Jewish refugees would have undoubtedly perished before Rome was liberated."[10]

The Italian Jewish community on April 5, 1946, sent the following message to His Holiness, Pius XII: "The delegates of the Congress of the Italian Jewish Communities, held in Rome for the first time after the Liberation, feel that it is imperative to extend reverent homage to Your Holiness, and to express the most profound gratitude that animates all Jews for your fraternal humanity toward them during the years of persecution when their lives were endangered by Nazi-Fascist barbarism....The Jews will perpetually remember how much, under the direction of the Pontiff, the Church did for them during that terrible period."

Israel Anton Zolli

Claims that Pope Pius XII never instructed religious to protect Jews during the war are contradicted by the Chief Rabbi of Rome, Israel Anton Zolli.

The American Hebrew in New York published an interview with Rabbi Zolli on July 14, 1944. Having been hidden in the Vatican during the German occupation of Rome, he emphatically stated: "The Vatican has always helped the Jews and the Jews are very grateful for the charitable work of the Vatican, all done without distinction of race."

After the war, Rabbi Zolli converted to Catholicism and wrote his memoirs, *Before the Dawn* (1954). He devoted an entire chapter in his memoirs to the German occupation of Rome and praised the Pope's leadership: "The Holy Father sent by hand a letter to the bishops instructing them to lift the enclosure from convents and monasteries, so that they could become refuges for the Jews. I know of one convent where the Sisters slept in the basement, giving up their beds to Jewish

The Chief Rabbi of Rome, Israel Anton Zolli.

refugees. In face of this charity, the fate of so many of the persecuted is especially tragic."

Rabbi Zolli was hidden in the Vatican. His wife and his twenty-year-old daughter, Miriam, were hidden in a convent. They were eyewitnesses of the deportation of Rome's Jews by the Gestapo in 1943.

Zolli was baptized February 13, 1945, by Rome's Auxiliary Bishop, Luigi Traglia, in the Church of Santa Maria degli Angeli. In gratitude to Pius XII, Israel Zolli took the name Eugenio. A year later his wife and daughter were also baptized.

In his book *Antisemitismo*, Rabbi Zolli states: "World Jewry owes a great debt of gratitude to Pius XII for his repeated and pressing appeals for justice on behalf of the Jews and, when these did not prevail, for his strong protests against evil laws and procedures....No hero in all of history was more militant, more fought against, none more heroic than Pius XII in pursuing the work of true charity!…and this on behalf of all the suffering children of God."

Sister Pascalina Lehnert

Pius XII was a humble person who did not want his many good works and accomplishments revealed. Implementing the Pope's charitable works as Nuncio, Cardinal Secretary of State, and Supreme Pontiff was Sister Pascalina Lehnert. She was his housekeeper from 1923 to 1958—the period from when he was Nuncio in Germany to his death—and served him faithfully, respecting his wishes.

In her memoirs she explains that one day Pius XII prepared an official protest to be published the following day in *L'Osservatore Romano*. As he entered the kitchen and stood before the blazing fireplace, he told Sister Pascalina that he decided not to have his protest printed and would now burn it. She objected and reminded him that it might be useful in the future. Pius XII said: "This

VATICANO is clearly visible on the side of this truck assigned to the transportation of refugees.

protest is stronger than that of the Dutch bishops. I thought about filing it, but if the Nazis come and find it, what will happen to the Catholics and Jews in Germany? No, it is better to destroy this strong protest." With that, he threw it into the fire. Instead, he ordered Amleto Cicognani, Apostolic Delegate in Washington, D.C., to have the text of the Dutch bishops' protest published and circulated in the United States.

Among the nine hundred pages of depositions for the beatification of Pius XII, Sister Pascalina clearly stated (*Processo Romano*, pp. 84–85) that Pius XII did not issue a condemnation of Nazism because the German and Austrian bishops dissuaded him from making additional protests that would undoubtedly irritate Hitler. Jews and Christians had suffered in the past because of Vatican pronouncements, and they feared increased retaliation.

"The Pope," Sister Pascalina wrote, "not only opened the doors of the Vatican to protect the persecuted, but he encouraged convents and monasteries to offer hospitality. The Vatican provided provisions for these people. The accusation that Pius XII was indifferent to the needs of the victims is without foundation. He ordered me to spend his inheritance and personal funds to provide for those who wished to leave Italy and go to Canada, Brazil or elsewhere. Note that $800 was needed for each person who emigrated. Many times the Pope would ask me to deliver a sealed envelope, containing $1,000 or more, to Jewish families" (Session CLXIII, March 17, 1972). In general, while begging for help, the Jews who were in contact with Pope Pius XII insisted that he avoid any public action.

CHAPTER VII

Documents of the Holy See

For documents about World War II and the Holocaust, one need only consult the eleven volumes (Volume II is in two tomes) of Vatican documents. Pope Paul VI in 1963 ordered the opening of the Vatican archives. He selected Jesuit church historians: Pierre Blet, Angelo Martini, Burkhart Schneider, and Robert A. Graham. Their combined scholarship produced *Actes et Documents du Saint Siège relatifs à la Seconde Guerre Mondiale*, published between 1965 and 1981 by Città del Vaticano. Historian Eamon Duffy stated that this publication "decisively established the falsehood of Hochhuth's specific allegations."

The documents show the groundlessness of the attacks on Pius XII regarding his so-called "silence" and establish once and for all the action of the Holy See in sympathy with the victims of the war and in opposition especially to the racial persecutions.

During the winter of 1965, Father Robert Leiber, who had been for more than thirty years the private secretary of Eugenio Pacelli, disclosed the existence of drafts of the letters of Pius XII to the German bishops. These personal letters best explain the Pope's instructions. They show objectively the true attitude and behavior of Pius XII during the conflict and, consequently, the groundlessness of the accusations against his memory.

There is no evidence that the attitude Pacelli is claimed to have absorbed during his years as Nuncio to that country was in any way favorable to the Hitler Government. Of forty-four major addresses in Germany, forty condemned some aspect of Nazism.

Pacelli comforted the Catholic Church in Germany, which was being persecuted by the German Government. His efforts—joining President Roosevelt to keep Italy out of the conflict; sending the May 10, 1940, telegrams to the sovereigns of Belgium,

Holland, and Luxemburg after the invasion by the *Wehrmacht*; courageously advising Mussolini and King Vittorio Emanuele III to explore a separate peace—surely do not suggest such a pro-Nazi attitude.

Neither does the accusation of "silence" hold up. What appears to be silence was, in fact, a concealment of action conducted through the nunciatures and the bishops to avoid or, at least, limit the deportations and persecutions. In many speeches and in his letters to the German bishops, Pope Pius XII clearly explained that discretion was exercised. Documents show he constantly opposed the deportation of the Holocaust victims.

Father Pierre Blet, one of the four editors of the *Actes*, stated that "a public declaration would not have been of any help; it would have accomplished nothing except to aggravate the situation of the victims and multiply their number....Without Father Leiber, we would not have been aware of the existence of the drafts of Pius XII's letters to the German bishops and the collection would have been deprived of perhaps the most precious texts to understand the Pope's mind. But all of those texts taken together do not contradict at all what we learn from the diplomatic notes and correspondence."

In these documents we learn that Pius XII emphasized to the bishops the need to warn German Catholics against National Socialism as an enemy of the Church—a risky move on his part even more so in a time of war. This correspondence, published in the second volume of *Actes et Documents*, confirms the opposition of the Church to National Socialism and the Church's compassion for the victims.[11] Already there had been warnings—disseminated by Bishops Faulhaber and von Galen and by many religious and clergymen in Germany—that culminated with the encyclical *Mit brennender Sorge*, read in all the German churches on Palm Sunday 1937.

Pius XII blesses the faithful in St. Peter's Square.

Message to the Cardinals

Pius XII addressed the Cardinals on the condition of the Church after the war. It was an earnest appeal for world peace:

"All are called upon to devote themselves to peace, each in his own office and at his own place....Nobody could accuse the Church of not having denounced and exposed in time the true nature of the National Socialist movement and the danger to which it exposed Christian civilization....Continuing the work of our predecessor, we ourselves have during the war and especially in our radio messages constantly set forth the demands and perennial laws of humanity and of the Christian faith against modern scientific methods to torture or eliminate people who were often innocent.... From the prisons, concentration camps and fortresses are now pouring out, together with the political prisoners, also the crowds of those, whether clergy or laymen, whose only crime was their

Mosaic depicting Pius XII praying in the National Shrine
of the Immaculate Conception in Washington, DC.

Smiling, the Holy Father greets his people from the *Sedia Gestatoria*.

Pius XII examines precious manuscripts during his visit to Capranica Seminary where he studied for the priesthood.

The Pope tenderly caresses the sheep in Castelgandolfo, his summer residence.

Pius XII at his desk in the Vatican.

Pius XII with
the bird he
nurtured back
to health.

WARTIME CORRESPONDENCE

BETWEEN

PRESIDENT ROOSEVELT

AND

POPE PIUS XII

PREFACE
BY

HIS HOLINESS POPE PIUS XII

The late Honorable Franklin D. Roosevelt, President of the United States, in his letter addressed to Us on the 14th of February 1940 clearly set forth the purpose he had in mind in sending his Personal Representative to the Holy See. It was that the one so designated by him would be "the channel of communication for any views You and I might wish to exchange in the interest of concord among the peoples of the world."

The correspondence published herewith and the observations and references to be found therein, brief though they be at times and occasioned by circumstances, show how well the appointment has served the purpose intended. Its full significance however was much more far-reaching than this, as may be gathered from a perusal of the letters themselves.

The fortunate outcome of numberless occurrences which arose both during the course of the war and in the post-war period, the solution of urgent problems, the interchange of important information, the organization of American relief which flowed in such generous streams to alleviate the misery begotten of the war, all these would have been well nigh unthinkable and almost impossible, were it not for the designation of a Personal Representative of the President and the magnanimous cooperation and achievements of His Excellency, Mr. Myron Taylor.

PIUS PP. XII

FROM THE VATICAN, *August 6, 1946*

Preface to the Pope's Wartime Correspondence with President Roosevelt.

fidelity to Christ and to the faith of their fathers or the dauntless fulfillment of their duties as priests. But we will not lose heart....

"May the Holy Spirit, light of intellects, gentle ruler of hearts, deign to hear the prayers of His Church and guide in their arduous work those who in accordance with their mandate are striving sincerely despite obstacles and contradictions to reach the goal so universally, so ardently, desired: peace, a peace worthy of the name; ...a peace that may stand out in the centuries as a resolute advance in the affirmation of human dignity and of ordered liberty; a peace that may be like the Magna Charta which closed the dark age of violence; a peace that under the merciful guidance of God may let us so pass through temporal prosperity that we may not lose eternal happiness....

"But before reaching this peace it still remains true that millions of men at their own fireside or in battle, in prison or in exile must still drink their bitter chalice. How we long to see the end of their sufferings and anguish, the realization of their hopes! For them, too, and for all mankind that suffers with them and in them may our humble and ardent prayer ascend to Almighty God" (Message of June 2, 1945).[12]

CHAPTER VIII

Pope Pius XII and the Catholic Church

Pius XII's pontificate left a lasting mark on the history of the Catholic Church. His life was one of action, inspired by profound piety. Understanding the weaknesses of humanity, the Pope brought consolation, peace, and encouragement everywhere. Striving to bring people closer to Christ, Pius XII instituted numerous liturgical reforms: the evening Mass, the new Eucharistic fast regulations, and increased lay participation in liturgical functions. The Eucharistic Liturgy was the source from which Pius XII drew strength and wisdom to lead the world.

Pius XII has been called the "Pope of Mary" for his great devotion to the Mother of God, evidenced in the infallible definition of the Assumption. The consecration of Russia and of the whole world to the Immaculate Heart of Mary, the solemn proclaiming of the Marian Year, the institution of the feast of the Queenship of Mary, and the proclamation of the Centenary of the Apparitions of Our Blessed Lady to St. Bernadette were also made by Pius XII.

There was a bond of friendship between the highly cultured Pius XII and Guglielmo Marconi, who installed the Vatican Radio Station. The Pope understood all the aspects of our complex modern age. "The Church," he said, "loves and admires the progress of science in the same way that she loves art and every other thing that exalts the spirit and is for the good of man."

Pope Pius XII's conversations with the world's leaders, replete with amazing insight and comprehension, have been recorded. Of him, Dag Hammarskjold, Secretary General of the United Nations, remarked: "In no part of the world have I ever encountered one possessing a more penetrating or complete understanding of the great problems of our time. The wisdom of his counsels will guide statesmen for years to come."

As early as 1940, the Vatican published reports on the Church in Germany and the slaughter of Poles. Catholic defenders maintain that the Pope knew what the Nazis were doing not only to Jews but also to Catholic priests and nuns, Gypsies, Slavs, and other groups being persecuted. His strategy of helping behind the scenes was considered by his contemporaries to have been wise. He enunciated moral principles, avoided provocations, strove for impartiality among belligerents, and issued information about Nazi atrocities through the Vatican Radio and *L'Osservatore Romano*. In addition, he implemented the most extensive relief effort during and after the war and saved thousands of Jews and other refugees.

Pius XII spoke out many times in a strong "lonely voice." He spoke in language the whole world understood. From Santiago, Chile, the sentiments of Jews and Catholics were adequately expressed on October 3, 1943, in *El Diario ilustrado*: "In these tragic days, our minds recall the elevated figure of the Supreme Pontiff, His Holiness Pius XII, proven defender of the cause of the persecuted, especially our millions of European brothers and sisters who are innocent victims of inhuman massacres and cruelties."

Throughout the 1930s and 1940s, the Vatican newspaper continued its condemnation of Nazism. Among the papal representatives defying the Nazis was Cardinal Pierre Gerlier, Archbishop of Lyons, who became an outspoken critic of the Vichy Government. Shortly after the Germans split France into the occupied north and unoccupied Vichy France farther south, Pius XII sent a secret letter to Catholic bishops of Europe to be read in all the churches, reminding the faithful that racism is "incompatible with the teachings of the Catholic Church."

The Catholic Church denounced the deportations and the treatment of Jews. Courageous churchmen defied Hitler. On July 16, 1942, when the police rounded up thirteen thousand Jews in Paris, the French bishops issued a joint protest: "Our Christian conscience cries out in horror. In the name of humanity and Christian principles we demand the inalienable rights of all individuals."

Campaign against the Catholic Church

The defamation and vilification campaign against Pope Pius XII continues unabated. Increasingly, many Catholics perceive reference to Pius XII's "silence" as an insult motivated by anti-Catholicism. In fact, there is a tendency to refer to Pius XII's "silence," with its obvious allusion to the Shoah, and apply it to Pope John Paul II, who has done more than any other world leader to combat anti-Semitism. Dr. Eugene J. Fisher, Associate Director, Secretariat for Ecumenical and Interreligious Relations, National Conference of Catholic Bishops, sent a letter to the editor of the *New York Times* (May 9, 2001) stating that this troubling dimension inserted into the Jewish-Catholic dialogue needs to be confronted. The phrase, "silence of Pope Pius XII," should be "placed in the trash heap of the discarded language of racial, religious and ethnic bigotry."

Pius XII defamers embraced by the media—among them Professor Susan Zuccotti—allege that there are neither written records nor reliable witnesses testifying to Pius XII's efforts to save Jews. They either ignore or misinterpret the massive evidence that exists.

A telegram (No. 2341, March 9, 1944) reprinted in the book *From Hitler's Doorstep: The Wartime Intelligence Reports of Allen Dulles, 1942–1945*, contradicts Zuccotti's thesis. Jews and other refugees were hidden in the pontifical palace in Castelgandolfo when the Allies bombed the village. Nazi soldiers with heavy military equipment were stationed there and exchanged fire that, according to Allen Dulles, Secretary of State of the United States of America, "resulted in the injury of about 1,000 people and the death of about 300 more....The Vatican protested the bombing of its territory."

I have sworn testimony from rescuers like Sister Domenica Mitaritonna, who wrote: "With joy we received the Jews as our guests....They were welcomed by the Superior who had been solicited by the Vatican to help them."[13] Many rescuers interviewed in *Yours Is a Precious Witness: Memoirs of Jews and Catholics in Wartime Italy* (1997) agreed that they were able to respond collectively to the plight of the Jews only because the Pope had ordered them to do so.

Dr. Eugene Fisher wrote: "Several years ago, while staying at the Sisters of Sion house in Rome, an elderly nun...wanted me to know that the Jews hidden in the convent were fed by a truck that came from the Vatican bringing food on a regular basis. The nuns could not have fed 200+ Jews for so long, of course, because of rationing. Indeed, together with the food delivery, there was always a card which read, *With the Pope's blessing for all*."[14]

Was Pius XII "Silent?"

The charge of Pius XII's "silence" with regard to the Nazis is simply not true. In his *Diary* regarding an audience with Pope Pius XII on October 10, 1941, Angelo Giuseppe Roncalli, Apostolic Nuncio in Istanbul, declared that the Pope's statements were prudent. In his Christmas radio messages of 1941, 1942, and 1943 following this audience, the Pope denounced theories that attribute rights to "a particular race." He revealed that "hundreds of thousands of people, through no fault of theirs, sometimes only because of nationality or race, were destined to die." In the book *Pio XII: Il Papa degli Ebrei*, historian Andrea Tornielli cites the Evangelical Bishop of Berlin, Otto Dibelius: "What this Pope did or did not do, what he suffered or did not suffer, and the conflicts he conscientiously overcame before God, can be judged only by one who has had such a responsibility, and has learned what it means to profess the Christian faith and the Ten Commandments while in the frightening atmosphere of a totalitarian state and controlled by such a government."[15]

Certain Polish bishops, exiled in London, called for stronger statements by the Pontiff, while those who remained in Poland and had to deal with the Nazis cautioned the Pope to refrain from "speaking out" against Hitler, lest his words be used as a pretext for savage reprisals. In a letter to Pope Pius XII, dated October 28, 1942, Archbishop Adam Stefan Sapieha stated: "It displeases us greatly that we cannot communicate Your Holiness' letters to our faithful, but it would furnish a pretext for further persecution and we have already had victims suspected of communicating with the Holy See."

Despite Pius XII's peace efforts, the Allies would accept nothing short of Germany's unconditional surrender, even though it meant prolonging the Holocaust. John Toland reported: "The Church, under the Pope's guidance, had already saved the lives of more Jews than all other churches, religious institutions and rescue organizations combined, and was presently hiding thousands of Jews in monasteries, convents and Vatican City itself. The record of the Allies was far more shameful. The British and Americans, despite lofty pronouncements, had not only avoided taking any meaningful action but gave sanctuary to few persecuted Jews. The Moscow Declaration of that year—signed by Roosevelt, Churchill and Stalin—methodically listed Hitler's victims as Polish, Italian, French, Dutch, Belgian, Norwegian, Soviet and Cretan. The curious omission of Jews (a policy emulated by the U.S. Office of War Information) was protested vehemently but uselessly by the World Jewish Congress. By the simple expedient of converting the Jews of Poland into Poles, and so on, the Final Solution was lost in the Big Three's general classification of Nazi terrorism."[16]

CONCLUSION

In his book *I dilemmi e i silenzi di Pio XII*, historian Giovanni Miccoli reconstructs the facts and presents the mental attitudes, maneuvers, and difficulties of the Vatican Curia during World War II. Miccoli states that the Vatican avoided taking a position that would violate its neutrality. By condemning Nazism, Pius XII would have endangered millions of Catholics and thousands of German priests. He would have jeopardized, as well, the safety of the Jews in Rome, which was the center of Fascist Italy occupied by the Germans. To take a position could have signified that the war would be transformed into a crusade. It meant going to battle with serious and dangerous consequences. Ultimately the results would block the action of persuasion, assistance, and peacemaking that was the role of the Pontiff.[17]

Pius XII was far from silent. In *Summi Pontificatus* (1939) and *Mystici Corporis* (1943), as well as in his Christmas messages and his June 2, 1943, address to the Cardinals, he clearly repudiated Nazi racist ideology. He ordered papal representatives to intervene in Belgium, Bulgaria, France, Greece, Holland, Hungary, Rumania, Slovakia, Spain, and Turkey to stem the deportation of innocent victims to death camps. He took great risks to protect and save as many Jews as he could by sheltering them in Vatican buildings and releasing monasteries and convents from the rule of cloister.

There is no proof that a formal denunciation of Hitler and the Nazis would have been of any help to the Jews. The Church would have been treated as an enemy power, and the Nazis would have invaded the Vatican and searched Catholic buildings everywhere for Jewish refugees. Pius XII's own assessment was: "No doubt a protest would have gained the praise and respect of the civilized world, but it would have submitted the poor Jews to an even worse persecution."[18]

The fact remains that Pius XII's voice was heard. He was the object of unanimous admiration and sincere gratitude. Who can deny that Vatican Radio explicitly condemned "the immoral principles of Nazism"[19] and the "the wickedness of Hitler," citing Hitler by name.[20] The London *Times* praised Pius XII: "There is no room for doubt. He condemns the worship of force...and the persecution of the Jewish race."[21] *The Tablet* of London reported that Nazi leader Goebbels issued pamphlets in many languages condemning Pius XII as a "pro-Jewish Pope."[22]

In *Pius XII and the Second World War,* Pierre Blet concluded: "Several years later Pius XII returned to these years of fire and sword in a speech to nurses given in May 1952. He asked the question: 'What should we have done that we have not done?' The Pope was saying that he was conscious of what he had accomplished to prevent the war, to alleviate its sufferings, to reduce the number of its victims—everything he thought he could do. The documents [the *Actes*], in so far as they allow one to probe the human heart, come to the same conclusion. As for results, to affirm that the Pope himself or some other person in his place might have been able to do more is to depart from the field of history in order to venture into the undergrowth of suppositions and dreams."[23]

The vilification of the person of Pope Pius XII and the denigration of our present Pope John Paul II affects the Magisterium of the Catholic Church. Today, Catholics should promote the truth about the Holocaust—an important contemporary issue. Both Popes are accused of "silence." The Vatican chastised the Anti-Defamation League for its ads in the *New York Times* and the *International Herald Tribune.* On May 18, 2001, in a letter to Abraham Foxman obtained by *The Jewish Week*, Walter Cardinal Kasper, head of the Commission for Religious Relations with the Jews, defended John Paul II: "To defame the Holy Father by attributing 'silence' to him is quite unjust and cannot go uncontested....It wounds our relationship." In August, historian Peter Gumpel, representing the Vatican, denounced the "slanderous campaign" against the Catholic Church and accused some Jewish historians of "clearly incorrect behavior."

Discussion about the Pope's silence continues despite evidence that Pius XII did protest the persecution of Jews, Catholics, and other victims of World War II. Paolo Mieli, a Jewish journalist, courageously defends the Catholic Church in the *Corriere della Sera*, April 26, 2002. Writing about the film *Amen*, produced by Constantin Costa-Gravas, he states that "it is absurd to describe Pius XII as an accomplice of Hitler or as having any responsibility for the Holocaust."

How can anyone continue to deny the countless "testimonies" by victims of the Nazis in favor of this Pope? In the French magazine *Reforme*, dated May 14, 2002, a Protestant minister, François Beaulieu, confirms the fact that the Nazis considered him to be "the mouthpiece of the Jewish war criminals." This new evidence contradicts the statements by Rolf Hochhuth in *The Deputy* and Constantin Costa-Gravas in *Amen*.

On Monday, October 6, 1958, Pius XII suddenly collapsed while working at his desk. Two days later he had a second stroke. On Thursday, October 9, 1958, the Pope suffered a heart attack and died.[24]

When Pius XII died, prayers re-echoed throughout the world. Tears were shed by millions of faithful. People in every walk of life had been inspired by him. Men, women, and children of every persuasion had visited him in the Vatican. His enthusiastic, bright eyes, combined with brisk step and swift movements, were contagious. His personal magnetism was a blend of casualness and dignity, warmth and affection, compassion and humor. His food was frugal and limited as he dined alone while reading the newspapers at breakfast and reviewing official papers submitted by his secretaries during other meals. Though born an aristocrat, he was an ascetic.

Tributes of love and gratitude poured into Rome. The Jewish community worldwide expressed its sorrow. "The world," President Eisenhower declared, "is now poorer following the death of the Pope." Shortly after Pius XII's death, an article in *The Jewish*

Newsletter (October 20, 1958) expressed the uniqueness of his extraordinary contribution: "It is to the credit of Pope Pius XII that…instead of preaching Christianity, as the Christian Churches had done for centuries, he and the churches practiced its principles and set an example by their acts and lives, as did the Founder of Christianity." Richard Cardinal Cushing of Boston expressed the esteem of the whole world: "Pius XII was a pastor, a good shepherd of souls, selflessly dedicated to the Church and to the greater glory of God."

Forty years after Cardinal Eugenio Pacelli became Pope, on March 18, 1979, John Paul II recalled: "I shall never forget the profound impression which I felt when I saw him close-up for the first time. It was during an audience which he granted to the young priests and seminarians of the Belgian College. Pius came to each one and when he reached me the College Rector, Monsignor Fürstenberg, told him that I came from Poland. The Pope stopped for a while and repeated with evident emotion 'from Poland'; then he said in Polish 'Praised be Jesus Christ.' This was in the first months of the year 1947, less than two years after the end of the Second World War, which had been a terrible trial for Europe, especially for Poland. On the fortieth anniversary of the beginning of this important pontificate we cannot forget the contribution that Pius XII made to the theological preparation for the Second Vatican Council, especially by his teachings on the Church, by the first liturgical reforms, by the new impetus he gave to biblical studies and by his great attention to the problems of the contemporary world."[25]

Through nineteen years of unprecedented violence and change (1939–1958), Pope Pius XII led the papacy in a ceaseless search for peace. He spread a culture of solidarity and peace, and enriched the lives of his contemporaries by witnessing to the values arising from the Gospel, demonstrating their dynamic fruitfulness and constructing a more just and peaceful society.

Herbert L. Matthews, an American journalist in Rome, called Pope Pius XII "a peacemaker and conciliator" in the *New York*

Times (October 15, 1945). Pope Pius XII's 1957 Christmas message ended with these words: "Peace is a 'good' so precious, so desirable and so desired that every effort to defend it, even at the cost of sacrificing one's own aspirations, is a 'good' well spent." His last public word was "Peace." On October 5, 1958, he ended his discourse to the members of the Latin Notary Congress exhorting his audience to do its duty with regard to the "conservation of Peace, which is desired by all men of good will." Documents confirm that Pius XII was indeed a champion of peace, freedom, human dignity; a pastor who encouraged Catholics to look on Christians and Jews as their brothers and sisters in Christ, all children of a common Father. He was a witness of love and the Servant of the servants of God.

At the start of his 1987 visit to the United States, John Paul II defended Pius XII during a meeting with Jewish leaders, recalling "how deeply he felt about the tragedy of the Jewish people, and how hard and effectively he worked to assist them during the Second World War."

Furthermore, he extended an invitation for all, Jews and Gentiles, to be united spiritually: "I hope that at the dawn of the third millennium sincere dialogue between Christians and Jews will help create a new civilization founded on the one, holy and merciful God, and fostering a humanity reconciled in love."

This is what his predecessor, Eugenio Pacelli, attempted to accomplish during and after World War II. Regardless of race or religion, whoever approached His Holiness, Pope Pius XII, was overwhelmed with sentiments of filial devotion and deep veneration. One no longer envisioned Pacelli the man but Pacelli the Vicar of Christ in the fullness of his mission. With acute wisdom and courage, Pope Pius XII dominated the tempest of his day and age, disseminated the truth of the divine law, and endeavored to restore love and peace among all peoples.

APPENDIXES

I. Ten Commandments for Peace

1. Peace is always in God; God is Peace.

2. Only men who bow their heads before God are capable of giving the world a true, just, and lasting peace.

3. Unite, all honest people, to bring closer the victory of human brotherhood and with it the recovery of the world.

4. Banish lies and rancor and in their stead let truth and charity reign supreme.

5. Affirm human dignity and the orderliness of liberty in living.

6. Give generously of aid and relief—State to State, people to people, above and beyond all national boundaries.

7. Assure the right of life and independence to all nations, large and small, powerful and weak.

8. Work together toward a profound reintegration of that supreme justice which reposes in the dominion of God and is preserved from every human caprice.

9. The Church established by God as the rock of human brotherhood and peace can never come to terms with the idol-worshippers of brutal violence.

Pius pp. XII

10. Be prepared to make sacrifices to achieve peace.

II. The Wisdom of Pius XII

For nearly two decades, in simple yet loving statements, Pope Pius XII addressed words of wisdom to the faithful. Among his papal teachings, for example, it is interesting to note the unprecedented official Catholic pronouncements on the subject of womanhood. On October 21, 1945, Pius XII called for Catholic women to enter public life: "She must compete with man for the good of civic life, in which she is, in dignity, equal to him." Pius XII's treasured words continue to inspire the faithful:

The Aged: "People are inclined to reprove the elderly for what they no longer do, instead of reminding them of what they have done and recognizing the wisdom of their judgments."

Art: "Art helps men, notwithstanding all the differences of character, education and civilization…to pool their respective resources in order to complement one another."

Conscience: "Christian morality must be taught to youth and inculcated in the youthful consciences by those who, in the family or in the school, have the obligation to attend to their education."

Education: "It is never too early to mold the character and habits of a child. Education begins at the cradle; and the first school, which nothing can replace, is that of the domestic hearth."

Family: "In the order of nature, among social institutions there is none that is dearer to the Church than the family.…Parents must give their children a wealth of faith and the atmosphere of hope and charity."

Harmony: "If three notes are sufficient to fix with their harmony the tonality of a musical composition, the song of spring could be condensed into three notes, the harmony of which brings his soul in tune with God Himself: faith, hope and charity."

Humanism: "Ideas, good or bad, guide the world. Some philosophers aim their views at projecting a ray of light on present day questions;

others disturb the winds and sow confusion, particularly among the fine intellectual youth who tomorrow will be called to guide the coming generation."

Love: "God's masterpiece is man, and to this masterpiece of love, He has given a power to love unknown to irrational creatures: personal, conscious, free; that is to say, subject to the control of his responsible will."

Matrimony: "In the life of a wedded couple an essential nourishment of happiness is their mutual trust in sharing thoughts, aspirations, worries, joys and sorrows."

Peace: "Nothing is lost with peace. Everything may be lost with war. Let men come again to understand one another. Negotiating with good will and with respect for their reciprocal rights, they will perceive that honorable success is never precluded to sincere and constructive negotiations."

Prayer: "One finds God in prayer. He is a kind Father who will open to you His arms and heart. If you are in a state of grace, you will see in the intimacy of your soul with the eyes of faith God ever present."

Progress: "It is a clear principle of wisdom that every progress is truly such if it knows how to add new conquests to the old; if it knows how to store up experience."

Reason and Faith: "The homage which reason renders faith does not humiliate reason but honors it and exalts it, for the highest achievement of the progress of human civilization is that it facilitates the path of faith as it evangelizes the world."

Science: "If it is the duty of science to look for coherence and draw inspiration from sound philosophy, the latter may not arrogate to itself the claim to determine truths which belong exclusively to the sphere of experience and scientific method."

The State: "The more conscientiously the competent authorities of the State respect the rights of the minority, the more surely and effectively can it demand of its members that they carry out loyally the civic duties which are shared with other citizens."

War on War: "If ever a generation had to feel deep down in its conscience the cry "War on war!" it is certainly the present one. Gone, as it has, through an ocean of blood and tears, such as was perhaps never known in the past, it has lived war's unspeakable atrocities so intensely that the recollection of so many horrors cannot but remain impressed in its memory and in the depths of its soul."

Womanhood: "In virtue of a common destiny here on earth,...there is no field of human activity that must remain closed to a woman. Her horizons reach out to the regions of politics, work, the arts, sports—but always in subordination to the primary functions fixed by nature itself." (Address to the Federation of Italian Women, October 14, 1956)

III. Chronology of Pope Pius XII's Life
1876–1958

1876
Born in Rome of Virginia Graziosi, wife of Filippo Pacelli, March 2.
Baptized Eugenio Maria Giuseppe Giovanni, March 4.

1880
Eugenio Pacelli entered kindergarten and then attended elementary school.

1886
Received First Holy Communion.

1891
Studied at the Ennio Quirino Visconti Lyceum.

1894
Entered the Capranica Seminary in October; enrolled also at Gregorian University.

1895
Suffered a physical setback, requiring him to live at home while continuing his studies.
Registered in the Sapienza School of Philosophy and Letters and at the Papal Athenaeum of St. Apollinaris for Theology. He received the Baccalaureate and Licentiate degrees summa cum laude.

1899
Ordained a priest, April 2.
Assigned as curate to the Chiesa Nuova.
Continued studies for a doctorate in Canon Law and Civil Law at the Apollinaris.

1901
Served as a research aide in the Office of the Congregation of Extraordinary Ecclesiastical Affairs.

1904
Became a Papal Chamberlain with the title of Monsignor.

1905
Became a Domestic Prelate.

1910
Represented the Holy See at the coronation of King George V in London.

1911
Appointed Assistant Secretary of the Congregation of Extraordinary Ecclesiastical Affairs, March 7.

1912
Became Pro-Secretary of the Congregation of Extraordinary Ecclesiastical Affairs, June 20.

1914
Became Secretary of the said Congregation, February 1.

1917
Appointed Nuncio to Bavaria, Germany, April 20.
Consecrated Bishop and elevated to the rank of Archbishop, May 13.
Presented his credentials to Ludwig III, King of Bavaria, May 28.

1920
Appointed first Apostolic Nunzio of Germany, June 22.

1924
Signed a Concordat with Bavaria, March 29, ratified by the Bavarian Parliament on January 15, 1925.

1925
Left Munich for residence in Berlin.

1929
Concluded a Concordat with Prussia, June 14, ratified August 14.
Recalled to Rome and received a Cardinal's hat on December 16.

1930

Appointed Secretary of State, February 7.

Became Archpriest of the Vatican Basilica, March 25.

1934

Presided as Papal Legate at the International Eucharistic Congress in Buenos Aires, Argentina, October 10–14.

1935

Spoke at Lourdes, April 25–28, as Pope Pius XI's delegate to France for the closing days of the jubilee year honoring the nineteenth centenary of Redemption.

1936

Arrived in the United States of America on the *Conte di Savoia*, October 8, for an "unofficial" trip covering some eight thousand miles chiefly by plane, as he made an in-depth study of the American Church.

Invited to a luncheon at Hyde Park after President Franklin D. Roosevelt's re-election.

1937

Traveled to France in July as Cardinal-Legate to consecrate and dedicate the new basilica in Lisieux during the Eucharistic Congress.

1938

Presided at the International Eucharistic Congress in Budapest, May 25–30.

1939

Elected Pope, on March 2, taking the name of Pius XII.

Received the papal tiara, March 12.

Issued his first encyclical, *Summi Pontificatus* (On the Unity of Human Society—an attack on totalitarianism—October 20, after the Nazis' invasion of Poland, September 1).

1943

Issued *Mystici Corporis Christi*, June 29.

Comforted the injured, administered the Last Rites, distributed money to those in need of food and clothing when American bombers dropped hundreds of tons of explosives on Rome, July 19.

Issued *Divino Afflante Spiritu* (Biblical Studies), September 30.

1947

Issued *Fulgens Radiatur* (14th centenary of St. Benedict), March 21.

Issued *Mediator Dei* (Liturgy of the Church), November 20.

1950

Defined dogma of the Assumption of the Virgin Mary, November 1, with a Papal Bull *(Munificentissimus Deus)*.

Issued *Humani Generis*, August 12.

1953

Signed a Concordat with Spain, August 27.

1956

Reformed the Holy Week Liturgy.

1957

Issued *Fidei Donum* (Future of Africa).

1958

Death of Pope Pius XII, October 9.

NOTES

1. Cf. Charles Pichon, *The Vatican and Its Role in World Affairs.* New York, E.P. Dutton and Company, p. 167.

2. Ibid., p. 147.

3. Cf. *Controversial Concordats*, edited by Frank Coppa. Washington, D.C., the Catholic University of America Press, p. 173. Pogroms were going on in Poland. The American Jewish Committee appealed (December 30, 1915) to Pope Benedict XV to use his moral influence and speak out against anti-Semitism. Eugenio Pacelli was deeply involved in the preparation of a pro-Jewish document signed by Vatican Secretary of State Cardinal Gasparri (February 9, 1916). This statement appeared in the *New York Times*, April 17, 1916, under the headline "Papal Bull Urges Equality for Jews." It was printed in *Civiltà Cattolica*, April 28, 1916, v. 2, pp. 358–359, and in *The Tablet*, April 29, 1916, v. 127, p. 565. Twenty years later, during his 1936 visit to America, Cardinal Pacelli met with two officials of the American Jewish Committee, Lewis Strauss and Joseph Proskauer, and re-affirmed Benedict XV's condemnation of anti-Semitism, promising to make its teaching better known. These facts are found in the archives of the American Jewish Committee and are documented by Naomi Cohen in her official history of the AJC, *Not Free to Desist: A History of the American Jewish Committee, 1906–1966*, Philadelphia, The Jewish Publication Society of America, 1972, pp. 180, 214–215, 578, section vii.

4. The *New York Times*, p. 6, col. 4.

5. The *New York Times*, January 17, 1939, p. 1, col. 3.

6. Cf. *Actes et documents du Saint Siège relatifs à la Seconde Guerre Mondiale* (Libreria Editrice Vaticana, vols. 1–11, 1970–1981, vol. 3 in two tomes), vol. 8, No. 329, nota 1, p. 481, and A. Rozumek, *Die Caritas des Vatikans*.

7. The *New York Times*, August 2, 1942, p. 10, col. 6.

8. *First Things* (magazine), August/September 2000, p. 22.

9. *L'Osservatore Romano*, January 5, 1946.

10. *L'Osservatore Romano*, July 30, 1946.

11. Cf. *Acta Apostolicae Sedis*, Vol. XXIX, 1937, pp. 149 and 171.

12. Libreria Editrice Vaticana, 1993, 2nd edition. Compelling documents vindicate Pope Pius XII. The evidence in *Actes et Documents* points to Pius XII's ceaseless activities for peace, He was against racism, nationalism, anti-Semitism, and war. His efforts were on behalf of the persecuted: Jews, the homeless, widows, orphans, prisoners of war. It is important to note: 1. The Holy See's February 9, 1916, condemnation of anti-Semitism, which Eugenio Pacelli (the future Pius XII), then working in the Secretary of State's office, helped formulate. 2. The January 22, 1943, report written by the Nazis' Reich Central Security Office, which condemned Pius XII's 1942 Christmas Address for "clearly speaking on behalf of the Jews" and which accused the Pontiff of being a "mouthpiece of the Jewish War Criminals." 3. The recently discovered Nazi plan, reported in the July 5, 1998, issue of the Milan newspaper *Il Giornale*, which described Hilter's plan to "massacre Pius XII with the entire Vatican," because of the "papal protest in favor of the Jews." The most recent followers of the anti-Pius XII myth, Susan Zuccotti (*Under His Very Windows*), Michael Phayer (*The Catholic Church and the Holocaust*), and David Kertzer (*The Popes against the Jews*) make no mention of any of these documents in their deeply flawed books.

13. Letter to Margherita Marchione, September 22, 2000.

14. Letter to Margherita Marchione, May 7, 2001.

15. Andrea Tornielli, *Pio XII: Il Papa degli Ebrei*, Casale Monferrato, Edizioni Piemme, 2001, p. 199.

16. John Toland, *Adolf Hitler*, Doubleday, New York, 1976, pp. 760–761.

17. Giovanni Miccoli, Milan, Rizzoli, 2000, p. 407.

18. Quoted by Joseph L. Lichten in his Introduction to Graham, *Pius XII's Defense of Jews and Others*, pp. 2–3. See also Lapide, *Three Popes and the Jews*, p. 247.

19. October 15, 1940.

20. March 30, 1941.

21. October 1, 1942.

22. October 24, 1942.

23. Paulist Press, 1997.

24. When Pius XII died, Padre Pio was consoled "by a vision of the former Pontiff in his heavenly home," according to Padre Agostino (*Diario*, p. 225). On May 26, 2002, Elena Rossignani Pacelli confirmed this statement. With her mother, the Pope's sister Elisabetta, she visited Padre Pio, who spoke about this vision. Referring to Pius XII's sanctity in his letter to Margherita Marchione (February 22, 2001), Bernard Tiffany quoted the following letter from Padre Pio's secretary, Reverend Dominic Meyer, O.F.M., Cap.: "Padre Pio told me he saw the Pope in Heaven during his Mass. And many miracles have been attributed to His intercession in various parts of the world (June 30, 1959)." One of the most charismatic figures of the twentieth century, Padre Pio, a mystic from Pietrelcina, in the province of Benevento, Italy, was beatified on May 2, 1999, and canonized on June 16, 2002.

25. General audience of April 28, 1999. No Pope throughout history did more than Pope John Paul II to create closer relations with the Jewish community, to oppose anti-Semitism, and to make certain that the evils of the Holocaust never occur again. Relations between the Catholic Church and Jewish people are marked by mutual respect and understanding. Pope John Paul II visited the Chief Rabbi at the Synagogue in Rome in 1986 and declared that "the Jews are our dearly beloved brothers," and indeed "our elder brothers in faith." He requested forgiveness for past sins by Christians against Jews. He established full diplomatic relations between the Holy See and the State of Israel. A survivor of both Nazi and Communist oppression himself, John Paul II has consistently praised Pope Pius XII for his heroic leadership during World War II and led the cause for his canonization.

Praise for
Other Books on Pius XII

BY

Margherita Marchione

Yours Is a Precious Witness
Memoirs of Jews and Catholics
in Wartime Italy

"...a remarkable achievement."
—POST-GAZETTE (Boston)

"It tells a story that needs to be told and tells it well. It is 'must' reading for general readers, teachers and students, Jewish and Christian alike."
—Dr. Eugene J. Fisher, Associate Director of Ecumenical and Interreligious Affairs, U.S. Conference of Catholic Bishops, and Advisor to the Holy See's Commission on Religious Relations with the Jews

"...an important and revealing work. And it is a cornucopia of quotable quotes."
—THE CATHOLIC REGISTER (Toronto)

"Your work...is a testimony of the charity offered by the church and Pope Pius XII. May it be a source of meditation for those who insist on misrepresenting the truth."
—Oscar Luigi Scalfaro, President of the Republic of Italy

Pope Pius XII
Architect for Peace

"...a truly valuable treasury of fascinating historical material....It is impossible in a short article to do justice to this great work."

—THE IRISH CATHOLIC (Dublin)

"...perhaps the most inestimable contribution made by the present volume is more than 100 pages of documents from the era under study...."

—THE CATHOLIC ADVOCATE and THE BEACON
(Fr. Peter Stravinskas)

"Sister Margherita Marchione has, in the media when the career of Pius XII was an issue, shown thorough scholarship and admirable clarity in expression. It is a delight, therefore, to welcome a full-length study, especially confronting expertly the campaign of falsification directed against the great Pope....a work to secure at any cost and to treasure."

—THE CATHOLIC HISTORICAL REVIEW

"...a spirited defense..."   —REVIEW FOR RELIGIOUS

"...another magnificently researched book...highly recommended reading..."

—UNIONE (newspaper), Italian Sons and Daughters of America

Consensus and Controversy
Defending Pope Pius XII

"Following up on the arguments in her earlier books, Sr. Marchione here provides many facts to refute the recent charges that Pius XII failed to do what he should have done to prevent or contain the Holocaust. To her credit, she defends the great pope who by his prudent and courageous action did far more to save Jewish lives from Hitler's 'final solution' than any other person on earth."

—Avery Cardinal Dulles, S.J.

"Sr. Margherita does an excellent job...."

—THE SOUTHERN CROSS

"...laudable...Certainly, Sister Margherita leaves no stone unturned in marshaling her evidence....superior documentation..."

—CATHOLIC HISTORICAL REVIEW

Shepherd of Souls
A Pictorial Life of Pope Pius XII

"This beautiful pictorial book of Pope Pius XII captured his humanity in a way that cold words never could. It is a treasured memory of the great Pope Pacelli who led the Church with holiness, wisdom and courage during the dark years of war and the following years of great turmoil."
—Most Reverend Joseph A. Fiorenza,
Bishop of Galveston-Houston

"Among the first to answer the modern critics of Pius XII, Sister Margherita Marchione has re-assessed the Papacy's role during World War II. In a field filled with biased historians who hide behind the façade of 'objectivity,' she is refreshingly honest and declares her unambiguous support for Pius XII at the outset of all her books. In her judgment, not only has the wartime Pontiff been defamed, but there is more than enough evidence to prove that he was a genuine saint."
—William Doino, Jr., Writer, INSIDE THE VATICAN magazine

"...she distills years of study into a short, approachable text augmented with an excellent collection of photographs of Pius and his times....This book should be in every Catholic parish library, school, and, indeed, home."
—Eugene J. Fisher, Associate Director of Ecumenical and
Interreligious Affairs, U.S. Conference of Catholic Bishops,
and Advisor to the Holy See's Commission
on Religious Relations with the Jews

"Shepherd of Souls should be in every Catholic parish library."
—THE SOUTHERN CROSS, Cape Town, South Africa

Teacher Resource

A Study Guide for *Man of Peace* is available at no cost. Receive your free copy by writing to Customer Service, Paulist Press, 997 Macarthur Blvd., Mahwah, New Jersey 07430. You may also download a copy free at our website at www.paulistpress.com. Type in *Man of Peace* in the search engine and follow the link to the study guide.